# HELP –

## There's a Computer in My Classroom!

*Other titles of interest*

Speaking Frames – Year 3    1-84312-109-3
Speaking Frames – Year 4    1-84312-110-7
Speaking Frames – Year 5    1-84312-111-5
Speaking Frames – Year 6    1-84312-112-3

Creative History Activity Packs
Jane Bower

Creative Science Activity Packs
G. Alan Revill

Scientific Enquiry Activity Pack
Practical Tasks for Years 5 and 6
John Stringer
1-84312-026-7

Scientific Enquiry Activity Pack
Practical Tasks for Years 3 and 4
John Stringer
1-84312-108-5

Activities for Children with Mathematical Learning Difficulties
Mel Lever

Number 1-85346-948-3
Shape and Space 1-85346-949-1
Measures and Handling Data 1-85346-950-5

# HELP –
## There's a Computer in My Classroom!

A very practical guide for teachers

**Alison Ball**

 **David Fulton** Publishers

David Fulton Publishers Ltd
The Chiswick Centre, 414 Chiswick High Road, London W4 5TF

www.fultonpublishers.co.uk

First published in Great Britain in 2004 by David Fulton Publishers
10 9 8 7 6 5 4 3 2 1

Note: The right of the author to be identified as the author of this work has been asserted by her in accordance with the Copyright, Designs and Patents Act 1988.

David Fulton Publishers is a division of Granada Learning Limited, part of the Granada plc.

*British Library Cataloguing in Publication Data*
A catalogue record for this book is available from the British Library.

ISBN 1–84312–119–0

**Acknowledgement**
Screen shots used by permission of Microsoft Corporation.

Typeset by FiSH Books, London
Printed and bound in Spain

# Contents

# Introduction

This book aims to help adults and children make the most out of the computer(s) in the classroom. The demands of the curriculum can squeeze out time to organise this valuable tool. By spending time customising the computer to meet the needs of the class and curriculum this valuable resource can come into its own.

For the purpose of this book **Windows 2000** is used. Other operating systems will be similar, and many of the principles will be the same. There are different ways of completing many of the actions, and it is not possible to share all of these. Shortcut keys are not indicated in this book but can be found at:

http://support.microsoft.com
http://www.labmice.net/articles/keyboard.htm

**Click:** Where the term 'click' is used in the text, this refers to placing the pointer as indicated and clicking with the left mouse button. Some instructions specifically state whether the left or right mouse button is to be used.

**Don't work through the book page by page** – it isn't that sort of book. Each chapter focuses on one or two computer techniques whilst managing a particular aspect of the computer. Choose the most relevant chapters to start with, using it as a reference book. Where appropriate, there are cross-references to other chapters.

**Website addresses** are correct at the time of going to print. These do change as some are taken offline.

**Maintain the computer at least once a term** – essential maintenance is easily managed. Y5 and Y6 children can be trained to carry out some of these tasks. These techniques will also help to maintain speed and efficiency.

# Managing the use of the computer

# CHAPTER 1

# Rules for using the class computer

This chapter sets out some ideas for establishing rules and procedures for using the classroom computer. These would easily apply to any computers within the school.

It is important to have rules for using the computer, just as it is important for the children to have class rules. They need to learn from an early age that computers are electrical machines. As such, they need to be looked after in order to make them last!

It is better to leave the computer on all day than to continually turn it on and off at the beginning and end of each session/lesson, as this is what causes the most wear to the actual components of the computers. Power it up at the beginning of each day, and then just turn off the monitor when it is not in use.

Obviously, it is good practice to talk through and develop the rules with the children in class. Here are some thoughts on the points that should be covered. These would be in the agreed wording: class, age and skill appropriate.

● Respect others in the class by making sure the computer is ready for them – only touch the computer when it is your go!

● Only turn the computer on or off if the teacher tells you to.

● If the computer does something you are not sure about, ask an adult.

● Work quietly and sensibly on the computer.

● Save your work in a suitable place – either in your own folder or on your own floppy disc or CD ROM.

● Save your work as soon as you have started. Keep saving as you work: REMEMBER Ctrl + S.

● If the computer crashes tell an adult.

● The computer has been set up so it is easy to work at. Only change things if your teacher allows you.

● If you are working at the computer, remember others may be waiting for a turn! Work as quickly as you can to complete the task.

● Help others who are working on the computer by leaving them alone. Only help them if the teacher says you can.

● When working with a partner or as part of a group share the computer! People learn by using their own skills – help each other by making sure you each have a go at typing, playing or drawing.

- Print only one copy of your work unless told otherwise.
- Do not wait while the computer is printing. Save and close your file and tell the teacher so someone else can start working.
- If you are working on the Internet only visit sites related to your work.
- The Internet is a huge library of information – it is important that you NEVER give your name and address if asked. Always tell your teacher if you are asked for any information about yourself.
- Do not download any information or games unless your teacher has agreed. If you continually save information on the computer it will slow down as there is less available memory.
- If you have your own folder on the computer make sure you delete any files you no longer need. Check with your teacher before you delete anything. If you have your own disc make sure you regularly delete unwanted files.
- When working at the computer, sit properly.

Here are some examples of posters that could be used as a starting point, with instructions on how to create them in the next chapter.

Foundation Stage: Class Rules

Foundation Stage and Key Stage 1:

Key Stage 1

# Our Computer Rules

## Everyone will get a turn

Work as quickly as you can

Save your work

Check before you print

## Look after the computer

Key Stage 2

---

### Computer Rules

Make sure we all get a turn by:

- Sharing the computer fairly.
- Working together quietly and sensibly.
- Leaving the computer settings as you find them.
- Ask if something unexpected happens.
- Check before you change the current program.
- Save your work regularly.
- Only print one copy unless told otherwise.
- Look after your health by sitting properly.
- When working on the Internet take care – never give personal details.

---

# Inclusion: organising groups and removing toolbars

It is important that all children have access to ICT – but it may be that within a class, for a variety of reasons, access is not equal. These next two chapters show how ICT can play a role in supporting inclusion. By customising the class computer, all children can have access, and that support is optimised for those who need it.

IT can play an important role in enabling children to access the curriculum in ways that would otherwise not be possible. For example:

- Access to a word prediction tool or word bank may enable a child to write a story of more than three lines or allow access to words which they would otherwise not use.

- Access to a template (e.g. science experiment) may allow a child to finish a task at the same time as his/her peers.

- Having a talking word processor may engage the child who has 'opted out' of any written task because of poor reading skills, or provide the more able pupil with access to information above his/her reading skills.

- Using a software program may develop skills in spelling or numeracy through regular practice.

- Changing the screen display may allow access to those with visual impairment among others.

- Altering the speed of the pointer/cursor or reaction time of the keyboard can prevent repeated letters and support motor control difficulties.

- General access to a computer may improve motivation or enable a child to concentrate on the task in hand.

## Organising and managing individuals and groups on the computer

Although it is important that all children get the chance to practice and develop their ICT skills, it is also important that the use of the computer is related to the lesson in hand. ICT should be used only when appropriate – and in some lessons and for some activities, ICT may not be needed.

Consideration needs to be given to group organisation. Pairing is the ideal, although, if necessary, three or four children may be able to work at one task if roles are clearly defined.

Pair the children up as soon as their ICT skills have been assessed or from previous records. This pairing remains throughout the year unless there is a need for change.

Pairings can be made by either:

- Pairing those of similar ICT skills
- Pairing a pupil with good ICT skills with one who needs help with ICT
- Friendship pairs
- Variable pairs – depending on the activity e.g. for Literacy, Numeracy etc.

The same goes for groups, although the best number to work at on screen is two, with three as the maximum. The main thing to remember is that all the children need to be able to see the screen, and to be able to work together productively on the task in hand – everyone getting a turn at the keyboard. The younger the children, the fewer in the group – although at any stage, the presence of an adult changes the group dynamics which can allow for more concentrated working.

Recording who has worked on the computer is obviously crucial to all instances. A simple class list, laminated, with space for the title of the activity (or activities) allows children to record when they have had or are about to start their session.

|  | The Three Little Pigs | ✓ | Addition game | ✓ |
|---|---|---|---|---|
| Angie |  |  |  |  |
| Ben |  |  |  |  |
| Dwain |  |  |  |  |

Having said this it may be that there are one or two children in class who would benefit from more time on the computer. If a child is only able to complete a written task by having access to ICT, it may be that this is allowed for in planning wherever possible. It will really depend on the class.

Another key to success is to keep the task specific and time limited (where possible). Here are some pointers:

- Use templates where possible so that children do not have to spend time on layout (see Chapter 5).
- Give precise instructions so that the task is short and purposeful e.g.
  - fill in as many of the gaps in the text as you can in 10 minutes,
  - draw a picture of a space rocket in 15 minutes,
  - complete the story in 15 minutes from the starter,
  - find out 3 facts about the Tudors from the following websites – you have 10 minutes,
  - get to this point on the CD and then stop,
  - complete one game and then let someone else have a turn.
- Make sure that the children are working on the computer – check regularly and with the understanding that they know their turn finishes if they are not working.

One simple addition to the computer is a set of headphones (or two or more with a headphone distribution box). This can improve concentration, and prevent other children listening in to the computer.

## Toolbars:

Remove buttons and toolbars that the children do not need to use:

To remove or add Toolbars:

Click on view

Toolbars

A Drop-down menu will appear,

simply click on the toolbar

to hide,

or add.

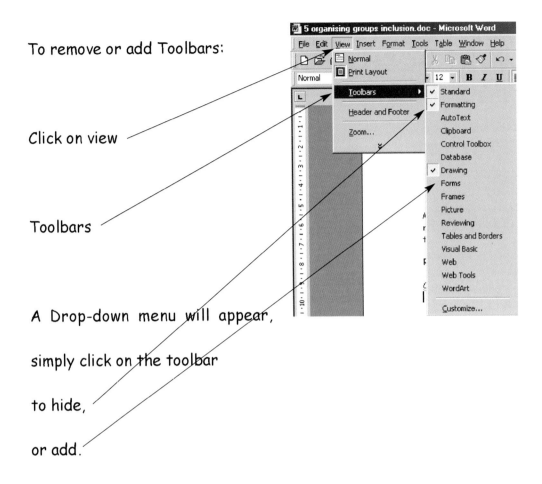

Removing all the toolbars focuses children on the task in hand, and can deter them from changing the activity.

Alternatively, add or remove buttons from the toolbar. (This is sometimes possible in other programs, and it is worth considering.) Children only need access to the tools they need for the activity.

**To add or remove buttons on the toolbar:**

Click on Tools

Then Customise

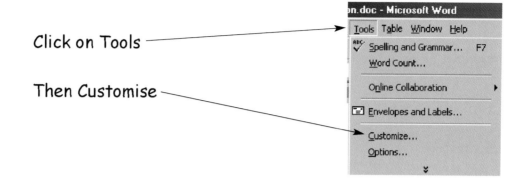

Toolbars tab allows you to view or hide Toolbars as above. For details on the options tab see below.

Click on the Commands tab

Choose the appropriate menu and the commands will change as appropriate.

Click on the command to be added and simply drag to the toolbar.

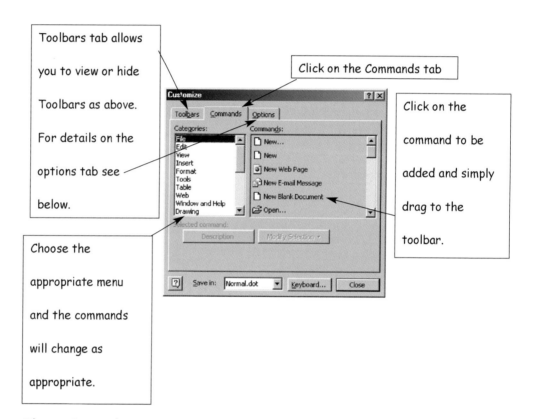

The options tab

Alter the toolbars to suit the needs of the class/task.

Click for Help here.

Some of these features can be useful. Large icons can be useful for those with visual or motor difficulties.

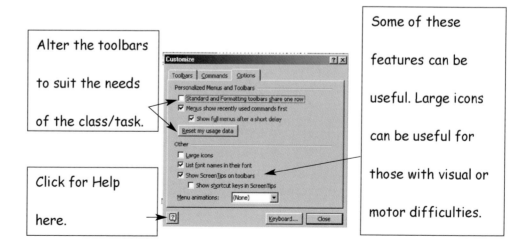

# CHAPTER 3

# Inclusion: left-handedness and Accessibility options

## Left-handed children

Some left-handed children can use the computer confidently with their right hand, but it is possible to change the mouse to suit the left-hander and they should be given the opportunity of exploring this option.

Click on My Computer on the

main screen.

Then Click on Control Panel

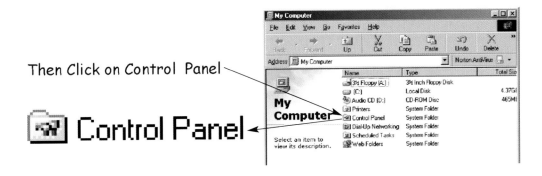

Double Click on mouse

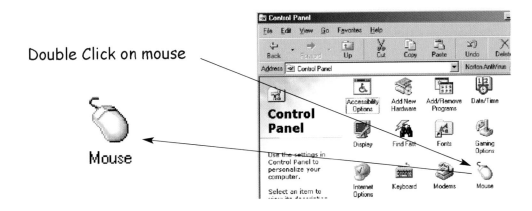

11

## Mouse buttons

The following menu will appear:

Click here to change between left- and right-handed mouse.

The speed of response can be changed here. This benefits children who find the double click command difficult.

For other tab options see below.

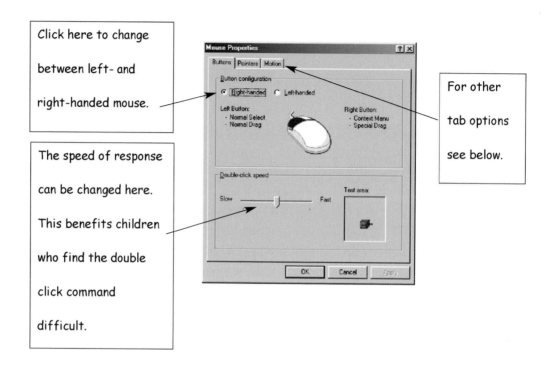

## Pointer/cursor appearance motion control

The Pointers menu allows for changes to the appearance of the pointer/cursor.

The Motion menu allows for change to the speed of the pointer/cursor and the option of showing a trail as it moves.

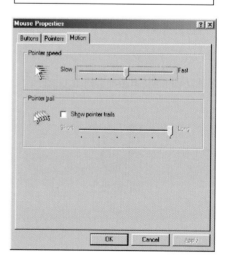

# Accessibility options

Although these are relevant mainly to children with special educational needs, they can have their uses for other children.

## To locate click on My Computer and Control Panel as above for the Mouse options.

Click on Accessibility Options ————

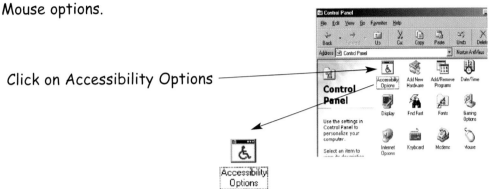

## Keyboard Tab

StickyKeys
For motor control this allows for pressing one key at a time rather than have to press two at the same time.

ToggleKeys
A noise is heard when certain keys are pressed. This can be a useful check that the key has been hit accurately.

FilterKeys
This allows the computer to be set to ignore repeated Keystrokes. This is useful for poor motor control or young children

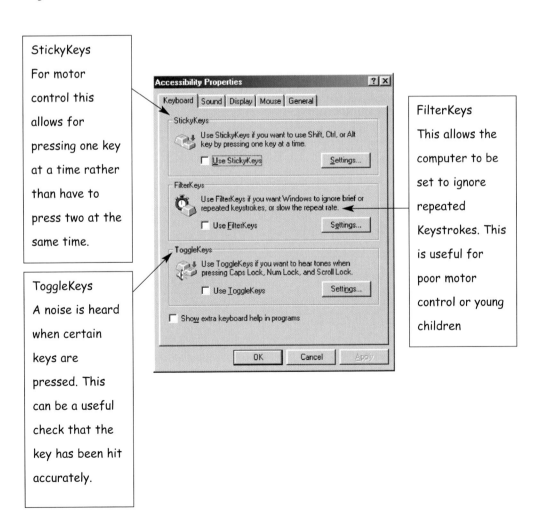

**Sound Tab**

This is fairly self-explanatory. It allows for sounds to appear with visual prompts. This could be used with children with hearing impairment, SEN or Foundation Stage.

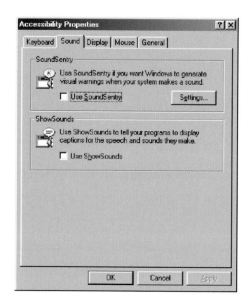

**Display Tab**

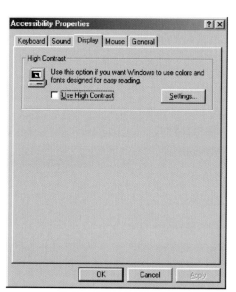

This changes the screen to High Contrast - useful for some children with visual impairment.

**Mouse Tab**

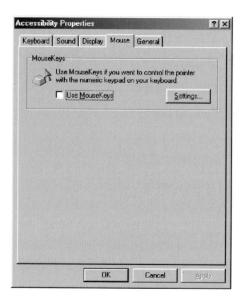

This allows the pointer/cursor to be controlled by the numeric keypad. This may be useful where a pupil is unable to use a mouse.

## General Tab

This turns the accessibility features off after a chosen time.

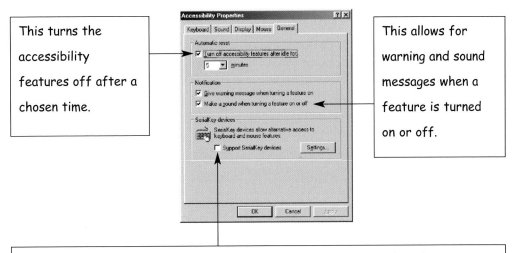

This allows for warning and sound messages when a feature is turned on or off.

Serial key devices allows for alternative devices to be connected to the computer and used instead of the standard keyboard or mouse. The Settings determine which connection is being used to plug in these devices.

The keyboard can also be altered under keyboard in the Control Panel:

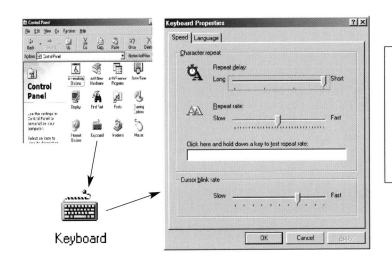

Keyboard

Here the speed and language of the keyboard can be changed.

There are a range of alternative keyboards and mice available, dependent on the age range of the class:

- The Intellikeys keyboard caters for a range of disabilities. It is a touch pad with similarities to the concept keyboard.
- Big Keys are keyboards with larger keys, and can be colour coded in lower or upper case.
- Touch screens are available although this is more specialised equipment.

- Rollerball mice allow children to move the mouse ball with their hand rather than have to move the whole mouse.
- Smaller mice are available which often suit smaller hands.

To find out about these, check out some of the specialist software companies and information providers:

| Abilitynet | www.abilitynet.org.uk | Information |
|---|---|---|
| Ace centre | www.ace-centre.org.uk | Information |
| Becta | www.becta.org.uk | Information |
| Don Johnston | www.donjohnston.com | Company |
| Inclusive Technology | www.inclusive.co.uk | Company/ information |
| Penny and Giles | www.penny-gilescp.co.uk | Company |
| SEMERC | www.granada-learning.com/semercindex/ | |

## Background colour and font

Some children find the 'white background, black font' hinders reading and other colours can give a better contrast.

To change the background:

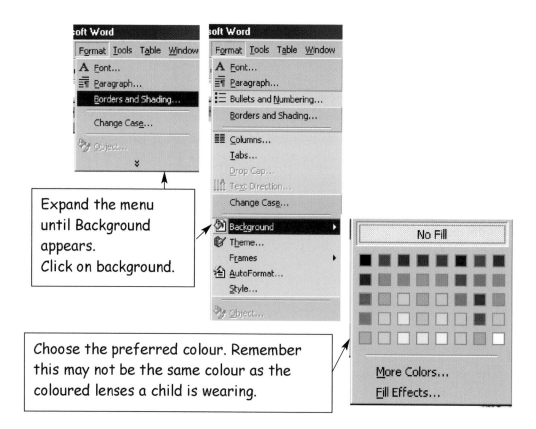

Expand the menu until Background appears.
Click on background.

Choose the preferred colour. Remember this may not be the same colour as the coloured lenses a child is wearing.

Font colour can be changed using the Format menu and Font or by the Font Colour menu on the Toolbar:

Check out other accessibility options on:

www.abilitynet.org.uk/content/factsheets/Factsheets-list.htm
www.granadalearning.com/special_needs/library/libra/3sl.jhtml

## Related issues

Two issues which have been debated in education and which can affect accessibility are:

### The use of capital or lower case letters on the keyboard

Initially the only option was to stick lower case letters on the keyboard – which eventually got worn away. Now there are plastic covers available that can be slipped over the keyboard: called Kid Gloves. These have an added advantage in that the keyboard can be changed during the school year once children are more familiar with upper case letters.

If a larger version of the keyboard is chosen (called Big Keys) it is also possible to buy a version with phonic cues on the keys e.g. apple for 'a'.

### Whether or not children should be taught typing skills

This debate impacts on a whole range of curriculum activities and timetabling and it is also difficult to see how teachers can teach typing skills if they, themselves, manage with one-fingered typing or are self-taught. However, it can be very useful for some children and can improve the speed of typing. Certainly, familiarity with the keyboard is essential for speed – and it may be that there is a way of allowing this option within schools.

There are some good Software programs around which are child-friendly and can support learning at the same time. Check out the software companies to see what is currently available. The Becta website has some pointers on this subject.

www.ictadvice.org.uk – look under 'How to teach Keyboard skills'

# Helpsheets for children: screenshots and Text Boxes

The illustrations in this book are all screenshots from the computer. These are easy to do and can be very useful in class, especially to support children working on the computer. The combination of keys for this process does vary slightly from computer to computer. If the process does not work the first time, try again, with the different combinations mentioned below.

## How to create a screenshot of a particular page:

Open the application or program to the page or screen. This page has been used as an example.

Press the Shift, Alt key and Print screen key at the same time! Print screen or Prt Sc is usually found at the top of the keyboard above the number key.

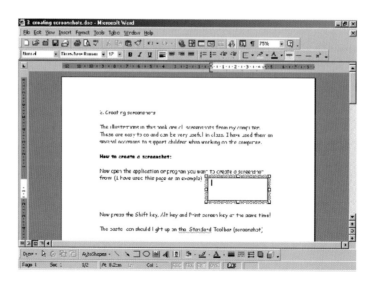

The paste icon should 'light up' on the Standard Toolbar.

Open a new document in Word and then click on the paste button. The screenshot should now appear. The screenshot will include the whole of the visible display, but this can be altered using the Picture Toolbar (see below).

N.B. The commands for screenshots may vary depending on the version of Word being used. If the above does not work, either use the method outlined below, or replace the Shift key with the Control (Ctrl) key.

It is often easier to paste the screenshot inside a text box so that it can easily be moved around the page – but that is a personal preference. See below for instructions on how to use text boxes.

## How to create a screenshot of a pop-up menu:

This type of screenshot requires a slightly different method.

Hold down Print screen and Shift, and then press Alt Gr (while still holding Print Screen and Shift).
Alt Gr is located to the right of the Space Bar. The Menu may disappear at this point but will still have been captured in the screenshot. Using the picture toolbar the screenshot can be cropped so that only the menu is showing.

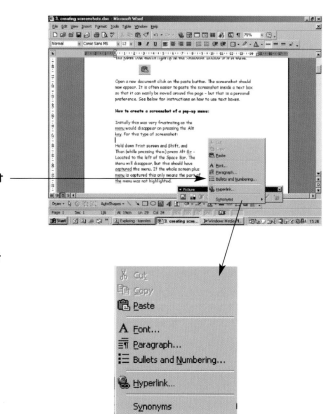

## Formatting the screenshot

The format of a screenshot can be changed – click with the right mouse button on the screenshot and a menu will appear.

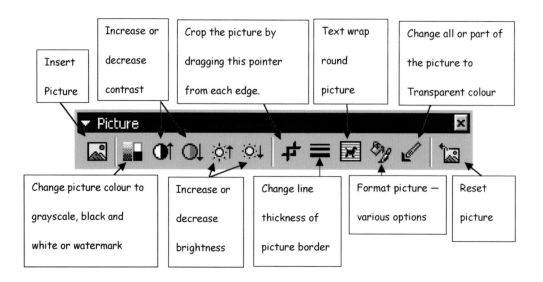

The above diagram has been used as a prompt for children when using pictures. A4 size and laminated, it can easily be stored and its life is prolonged.

The four picture colour options are shown here:

Colour        Black and White        Grayscale        Watermark

Grayscale is best if photocopying. Watermark can be used with pictures to provide the background for writing – either by hand or on the computer. See Chapter 10 for an alternative way of using this option.

## To insert a text box

Either click on Insert on the Standard Toolbar or the Textbox icon on the Draw Toolbar:

The 'I' beam cursor will change to a cross beam which is placed on the page. Then click and drag to size. Don't worry if it isn't the correct size at first. Simply click and drag on one of the corner handles to change the size.

To insert a screenshot, simply place the cursor in the text box and click on the paste button, Edit and Paste.

Both pictures and text can be inserted into a text box. Simply start typing for text and change the font and font size as normal. To insert a picture, simply click on Insert and picture and Clip Art (see Chapter 6 for more detail).

## Using screenshots in class

Screenshots can be used in a variety of ways:

- As a series of instructions for a particular program
- To teach children an ICT skill
- As a prompt for reference

They can be used on their own as below, or as part of a general set of instructions.

Here is an example of a series of screenshots created for a Year 2 class to teach them how to use WordArt within Publisher. Initially the class watched as the process was demonstrated. These sheets then served as a reminder while they worked in pairs.

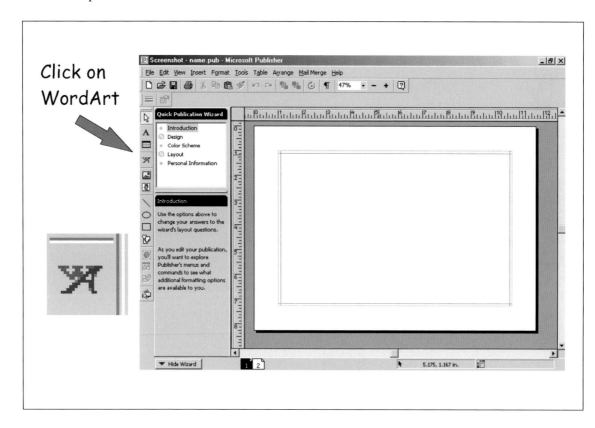

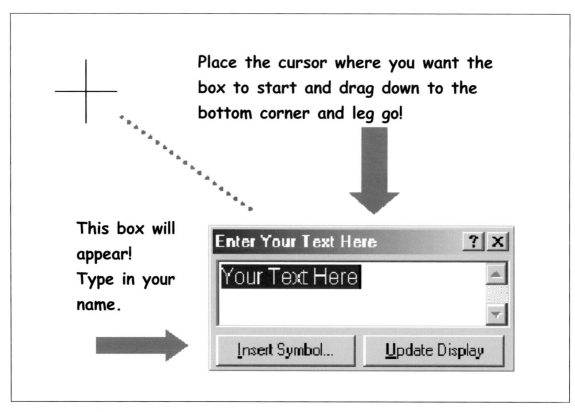

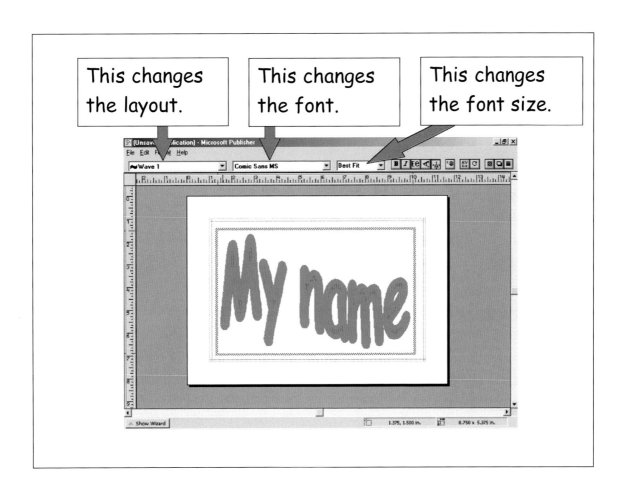

This changes the layout.

This changes the font.

This changes the font size.

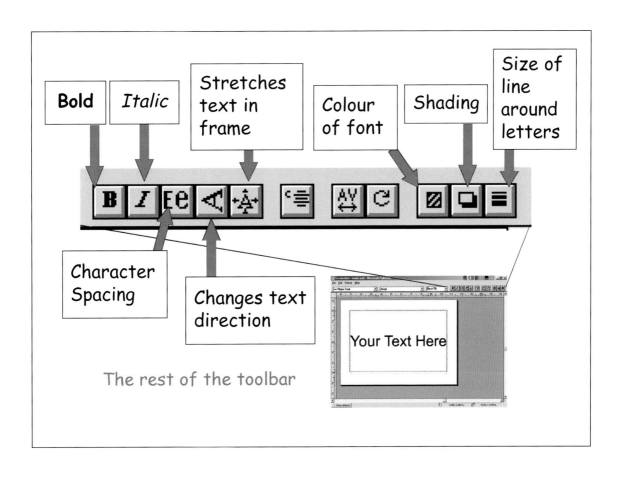

Bold

*Italic*

Stretches text in frame

Colour of font

Shading

Size of line around letters

Character Spacing

Changes text direction

The rest of the toolbar

Your Text Here

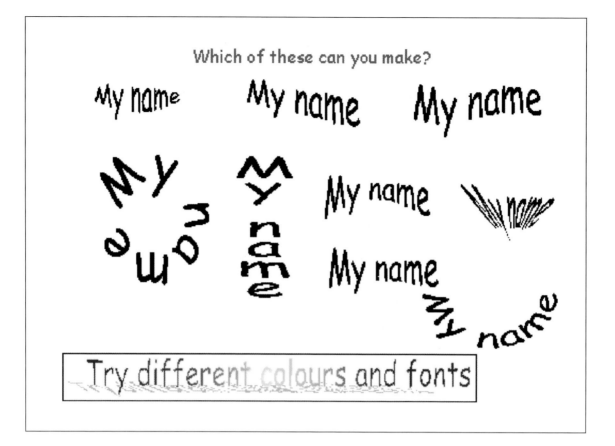

The children became very competent with this and were then able to transfer the same information to Word. It was presented in a series of A4 coloured sheets, ringbound so they could work through them like a book. They were done in landscape format so that the book could sit beside them as they worked.

The following two pages were used with a class of children working with the Drawing Toolbar. See Chapter 6 for more details.

Young children enjoy using the Drawing Toolbar and quickly become proficient in its use. As in the above example, the children watched a demonstration first. The first child was then supported while working through the activity and then peer tutoring was used to support the next child. This continued with each child reinforcing their own knowledge through teaching, as well as having the screenshots to refer to as prompts.

## Using the Drawing Toolbar

Check the Drawing Toolbar is showing:

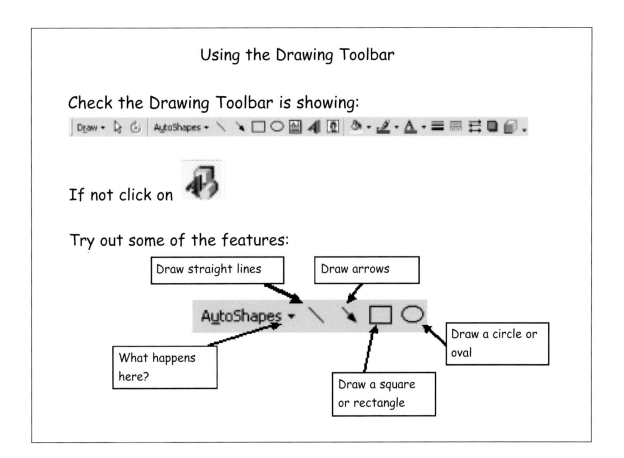

If not click on

Try out some of the features:

Draw straight lines

Draw arrows

What happens here?

Draw a square or rectangle

Draw a circle or oval

## Now check out these buttons!

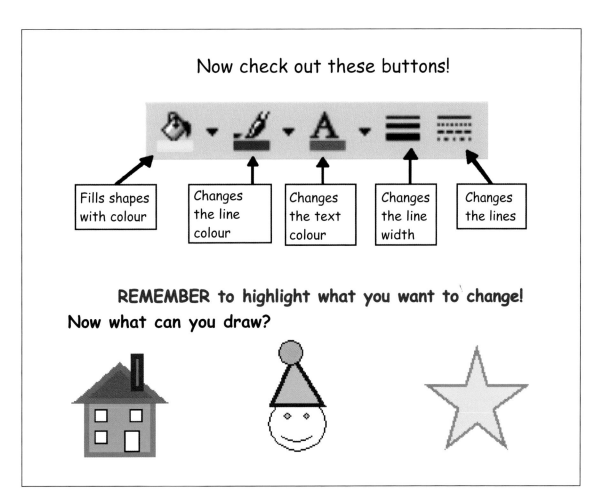

Fills shapes with colour

Changes the line colour

Changes the text colour

Changes the line width

Changes the lines

**REMEMBER to highlight what you want to change!**

**Now what can you draw?**

# Designing activities

# CHAPTER 5

# Creating templates and activities

This Chapter focuses on setting up templates for use in a variety of activities. Although based on Microsoft Word, the possibilities highlight what is available and can be used with other word processing tools.

For many children, being given a blank screen is difficult to cope with, particularly if their reading, writing or typing skills are poor. By developing a template they have a framework for their writing. A shortcut to the desktop display can be created when needed.

The range of examples here is not exclusive – hopefully the examples will provide a starting point for other ideas to match the needs of the class and year group/s under consideration.

## Template for writing a story:

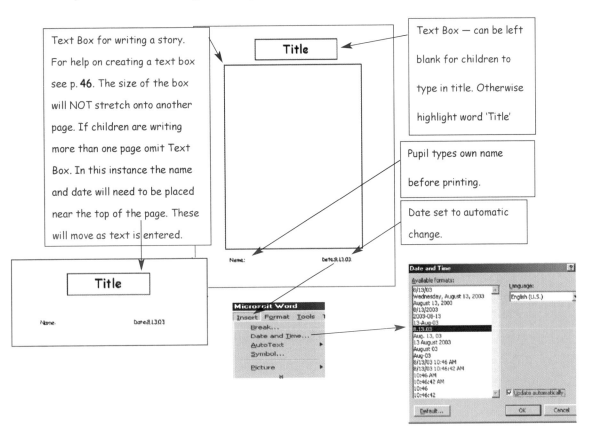

## Setting the template for pupil use:

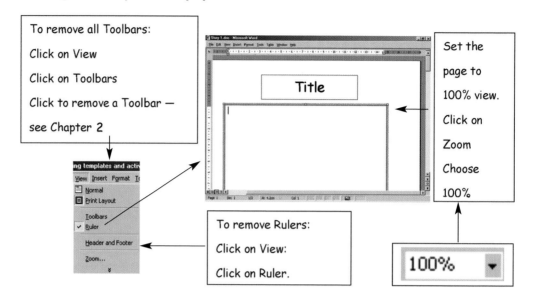

To remove all Toolbars:

Click on View

Click on Toolbars

Click to remove a Toolbar —

see Chapter 2

To remove Rulers:

Click on View:

Click on Ruler.

Set the

page to

100% view.

Click on

Zoom

Choose

100%

This worksheet can then be saved, and a shortcut created on the Desktop Display (see Chapter Fifteen for information on creating shortcuts). Deleting the word 'Title' allows for a printable worksheet if required, the undo button will replace 'Title' once the worksheet has been sent to print.

Click to undo

Save the file in a designated folder where it can be used as a master, and then save it in a work file where it can be accessed by the children. The master copy is a template which can be altered and saved as a different file, for other activities.

## Fixing text to the page

It is possible to fix (lock) text to the page, and still allow children to type their own work by using the Forms Toolbar. By entering the text that is to be fixed and then 'locking' it to the page, children can work on the master without being able to alter the main text.

Three features that may be confusing are:

- The text to be locked does not need to be highlighted. Simply type in the text and Protect Form will lock all the text to the page.

- The areas where text can be entered will appear as shaded areas, not as white, unless the Form Field Shading is altered. It may help to leave the shading as children can then see where they will be typing.

- The Tab key is pressed to move from one Form Field to the next, NOT the Enter key.

To fix a portion of text for story writing use the Form Field option:

Click with the right-hand mouse button on
a blank section of the toolbar:

The following menu will appear ─────────→

Click on Forms

And the Forms Menu will appear

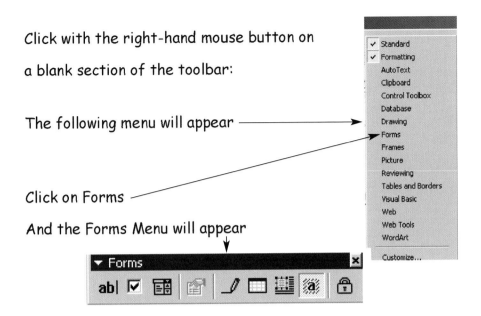

## Using Form Fields with story writing

Set up the page and type the required text.
Click on Text Form Field

and a shaded box will appear where the
cursor is placed.

Clicking on Form Field Shading
will change the colour to white.

Finally click on Protect Form to lock
the text. Children can only add text,
and are unable to change the locked text.

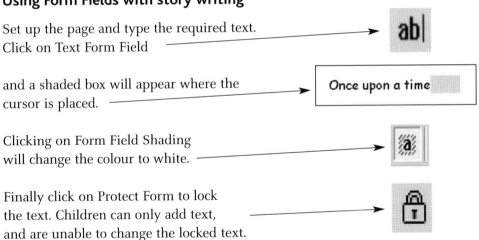

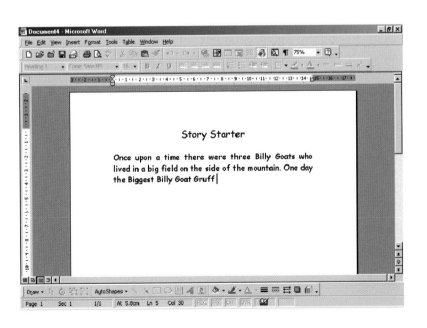

31

This also works well for Cloze procedure text. Simply type the text, clicking on space bar and Text Form Field each time a word is omitted. Then press space bar and continue typing. Once the text is locked using Protect Form anyone completing the activity cannot change the embedded text.

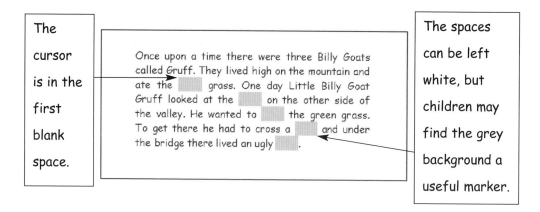

REMEMBER: After filling in a blank space, press the TAB key to move on to the next space, NOT the Enter key.

Text can be written in the Form Field which can then be altered as part of the activity. This could be useful where a particular word is to be targeted, e.g. 'said'. Children are asked to delete 'said' and replace it with a 'better' word.

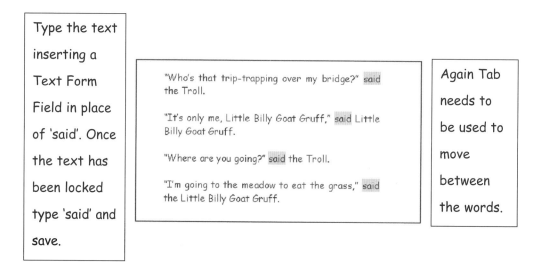

## Using the Drop-down menu feature

An additional feature of the Forms Toolbar allows for options to be added to each space in a Cloze Text so that a choice is available. Alternatively this feature can be used for multi-choice questions that are answered on screen.

Open the Forms Toolbar and enter the required text.

Click on Drop-down Field Form

A shaded area will appear

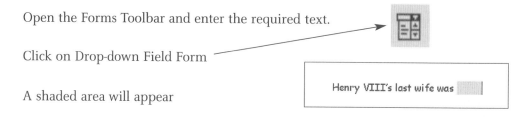

Click on Form Field Options

These features could be used for:

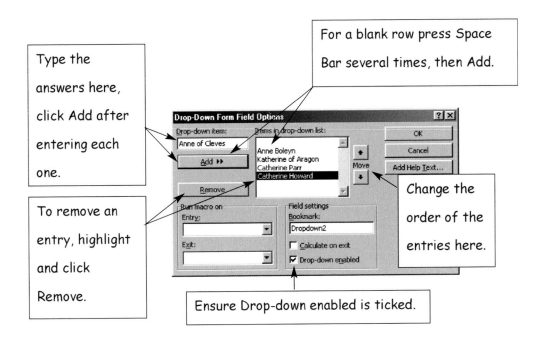

Type the answers here, click Add after entering each one.

For a blank row press Space Bar several times, then Add.

To remove an entry, highlight and click Remove.

Change the order of the entries here.

Ensure Drop-down enabled is ticked.

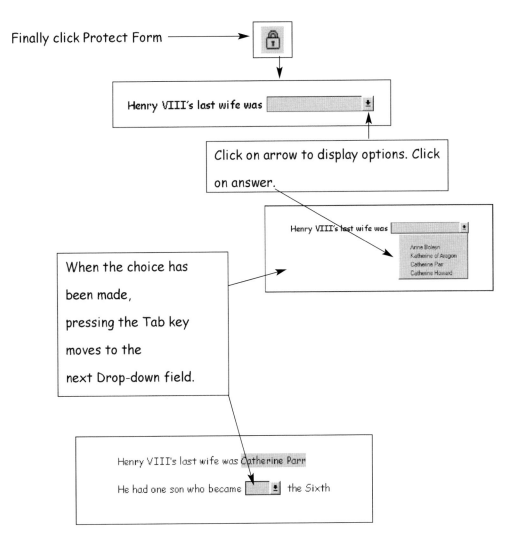

Finally click Protect Form

Click on arrow to display options. Click on answer.

When the choice has been made, pressing the Tab key moves to the next Drop-down field.

These features could be used for:

Cloze Procedure (Form Field)
Multi-choice Questions (Drop-down menu)
Options for Science experiment (Either)
Story writing (Form Field)
Changing target words e.g. said (Form Field)
Captions/Labelling for pictures (Form Field)
Missing letters (Either)
Answers to sums (Either)

# Using Clip Art and the Drawing Toolbar

This Chapter focuses on how to use Clip Art and the basics of drawing pictures, lines and shapes. It includes some examples of how these could be used for worksheets and activities.

## Inserting Clip Art

This is a useful skill as it could be used with any activity or template. Place the cursor on the page at the point where the Clip Art is to be inserted. (Placing Clip Art inside a Text Box allows it to be moved round the screen with relative ease, but this is a question of personal preference.)

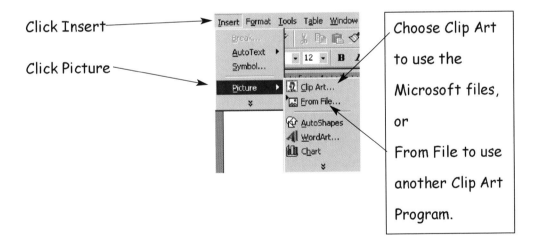

Click Insert

Click Picture

Choose Clip Art to use the Microsoft files, or From File to use another Clip Art Program.

Choose the desired picture and click Insert.

With access to the Internet there is a large library of Clip Art available for use – the main problem is locating a suitable picture. Use the search engine and remember to use American English – e.g. for 'jug' try 'pitcher'; for 'rubber' try 'eraser'.

Click on Clips Online

Choose Connect if not
Automatically online.

This will go directly to
Microsoft's online
Gallery of Clip Art.

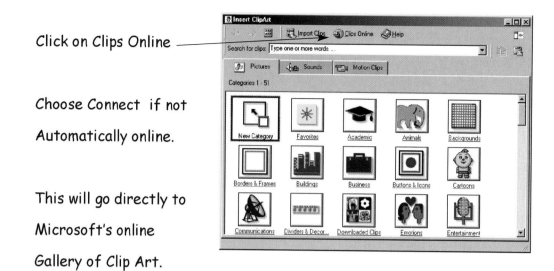

Select all the pictures to be used by clicking the box under each item and download from the selection basket. Disconnect from the Internet but DO NOT CLOSE Clip Art. Insert the pictures without closing Clip Art – simply click outside the menu to return to the document.

There is free Clip Art available on the Internet; use a search engine to locate this. Some of this is good and it is a question of looking and deciding what is useful.

**REMEMBER:**

With any Clip Art downloaded from the Internet or from a CD ROM there are copyright issues. It is OK to use Clip Art for worksheets etc to be used within class, but it is worth acknowledging the source if anything is going home. Check the copyright issues on the CD ROM or website to see if there are any issues that need to be considered.

Clip Art pictures can be edited using the picture format toolbar. Click on the picture with the right mouse button and the Picture Format toolbar will appear. See Chapter 4 for details.

## Picture Toolbar

## Drawing your own pictures

It is also possible to draw pictures, and even to write individual letters for handwriting! This is possible using the Drawing Toolbar.

Drawing Toolbar button

Drawing Toolbar

To use any of these features the object or text to be changed must be highlighted.

## Features of Drawing Toolbar:

To **Group** objects already drawn hold down the shift key and click on each object – Click Group.

**Grid** (see below)

**Nudge** and **Align** moves the picture

**Rotate or Flip** (see below)

**Text Wrapping** (see below)

**Edit Points** changes the Lines drawn.

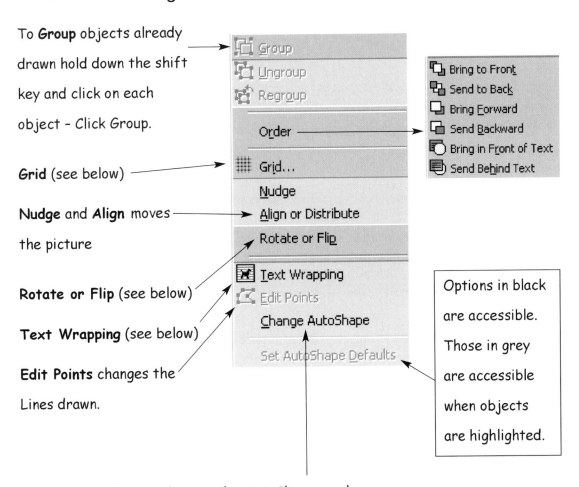

Options in black are accessible. Those in grey are accessible when objects are highlighted.

**Change AutoShape** – changes the AutoShape used.

Grid:

Using the grid options places some order on the objects drawn. This can be useful in spacing lines and when tessellating shapes.

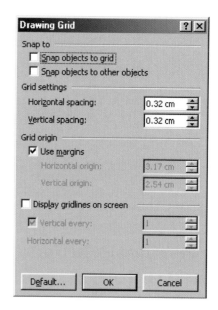

Rotate or Flip:

These options allow objects to be turned and flipped. Free Rotate is also located on the Drawing Toolbar.

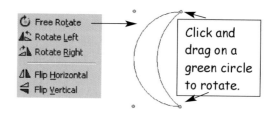

Click and drag on a green circle to rotate.

Text Wrapping:

This menu changes the relationship between text and picture.

These options affect both pictures and Text Boxes.

See Chapter 10 for an example.

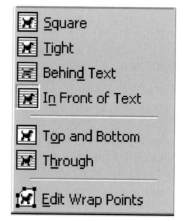

This feature can be useful when placing text and picture together to ensure that one does not obscure the other. Experimentation with the different options is the best way for finding out which options work best in any activity.

## Other Drawing Toolbar features

To group objects or ungroup them click on each object while pressing the shift key.

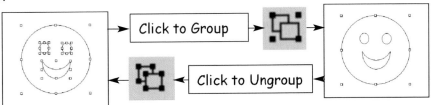

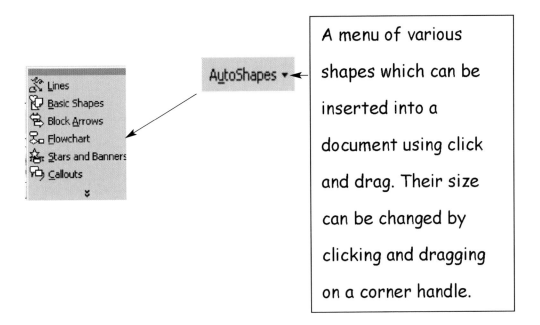

Select objects (point and click)

A menu of various shapes which can be inserted into a document using click and drag. Their size can be changed by clicking and dragging on a corner handle.

| | |
|---|---|
| \ | Use to draw straight lines |
| ↖ | Use to draw arrows. Place where the end of arrow will be and drag to the pointed end position |
| ▢ | Use to draw squares and rectangles |
| ○ | Use to draw circles and ovals |
| ▣ | Insert a Text Box |
| ◢ | Insert WordArt |
| ▣ | Insert ClipArt |
| ◔ ▾ | Fill any object or Text Box with colour — change colour by pressing arrow. This gives the choice of fill effects, colours, and preset colour options |
| ✎ ▾ | Change the colour of any line or Text Box border. The arrow gives the choice of colour and patterned lines |
| A ▾ | Changes the colour of text |
| ≡ | Changes the line style |
| ⋮ | Changes the line to a dashed style |
| ⇄ | Changes the style of an arrow |
| ▢ | Adds shadow to an object |
| ▱ | Changes a shape to 3-D |

# Creating handwriting sheets using the Drawing Toolbar

When using the Drawing Toolbar work in about 200 or even 500% as it is easier to line objects up, as well as writing letters or words.

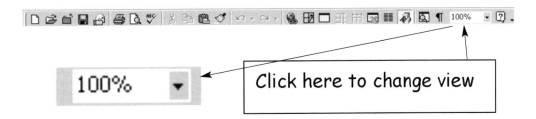

Click here to change view

## Handwriting sheet

This sheet is to be printed off and used as handwriting practice rather than on screen.

Start with a sheet saved as blank gridlines. These are made using the line on the Drawing Toolbar.

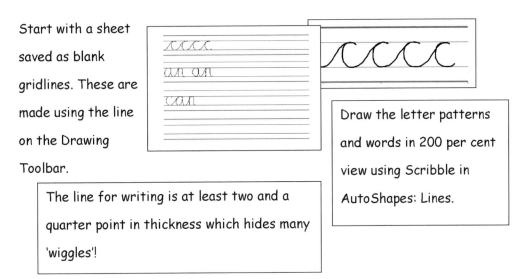

Draw the letter patterns and words in 200 per cent view using Scribble in AutoShapes: Lines.

The line for writing is at least two and a quarter point in thickness which hides many 'wiggles'!

It may take patience at first, but the line does not have to be drawn as a single line. It can be drawn in small segments.

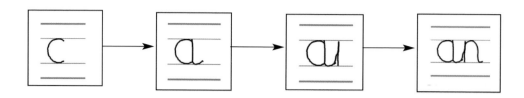

## Examples of Handwriting sheets:

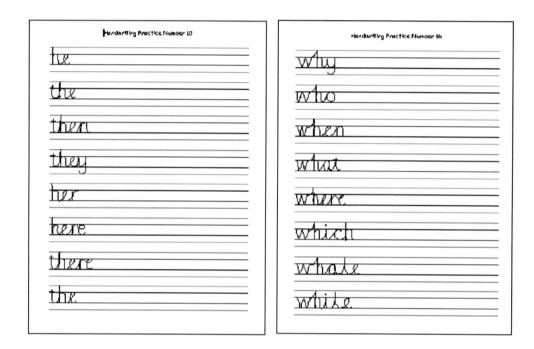

It is also relatively easy to create pictures using the Drawing Toolbar. These examples would all be printed off and used as paper copies rather than being used on screen:

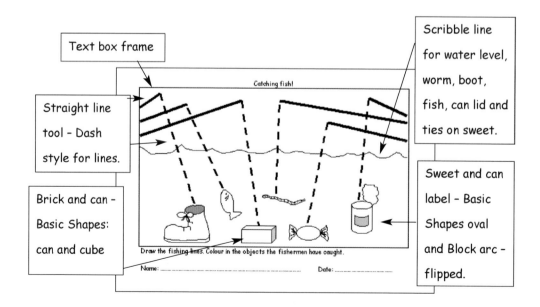

## Other examples:

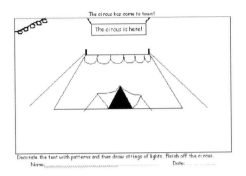

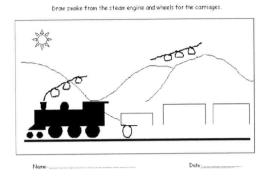

## Mazes:

| Created in a similar way starting with a series of rectangles. | 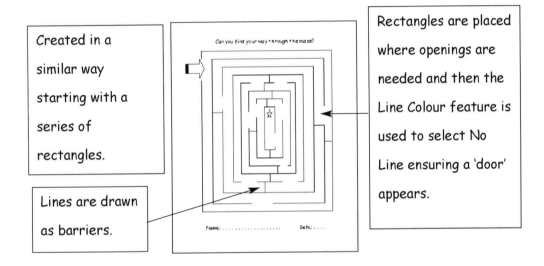 | Rectangles are placed where openings are needed and then the Line Colour feature is used to select No Line ensuring a 'door' appears. |

Lines are drawn as barriers.

The following examples could be used as on-screen activities if children are familiar with the Drawing Toolbar features:

## Visual Discrimination sheet:

| Draw a picture, group, copy and paste into the other cell of a table.  Ungroup and alter the picture. | 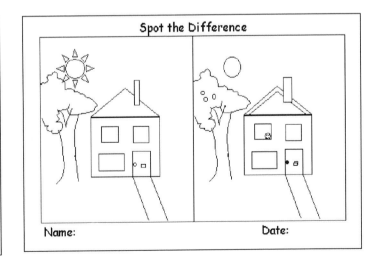 |

### Visual Closure sheet:

Draw the picture inside a Text Box. When copying and pasting shapes e.g. ovals for eyes, make sure the cursor is outside the Text Box.

Cover parts of lines using rectangles with no line colour.

Finish the picture

Name:

### Numeracy:

Title typed first

A Table is used: two columns, four rows.
This is stretched to fit the page.

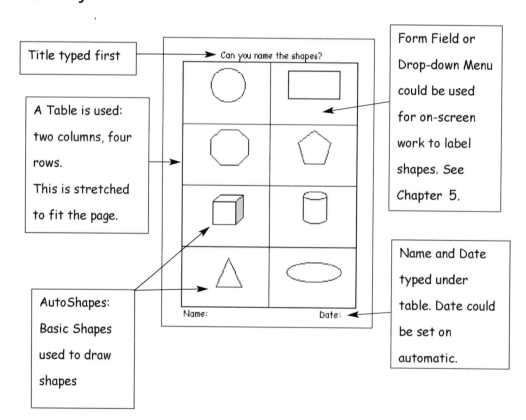

Can you name the shapes?

Name:        Date:

Form Field or Drop-down Menu could be used for on-screen work to label shapes. See Chapter 5.

Name and Date typed under table. Date could be set on automatic.

AutoShapes: Basic Shapes used to draw shapes

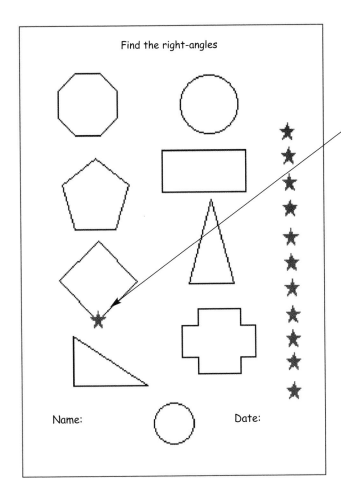

Find the right-angles

Name:                    Date:

Right-angles could be marked on screen with a coloured shape created by pupils, or by a set of shapes placed at the side of the page to be dragged and placed by the children.

# Interactive activities using Hyperlinks in PowerPoint

With the advent of new technology like interactive whiteboards, the use of presentation tools has grown quickly. Even without the use of a whiteboard, these tools can be successfully used for a variety of situations. Children can be asked to work through a series of tasks presented through this medium. No toolbars are present and the focus is all on the activity in hand.

PowerPoint presentations are made up of a sequence of screens.

When PowerPoint is first opened the following menu appears.

Click on Blank Presentation.

Click here to open a presentation already saved.

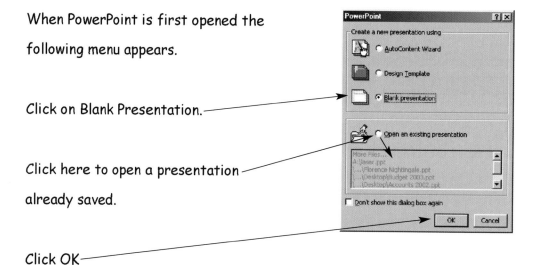

Click OK

A choice of layouts is available on the menu that appears.

In PowerPoint all text needs to be placed in a Text Box. There are a variety of options available including Blank. Choose the desired option and click OK.

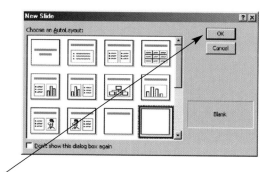

In Slide View the screen will look like the example here. There are various options for viewing the presentation as it is being designed.

Normal     Slide View     Slide Show

Outline     Slide Sorter

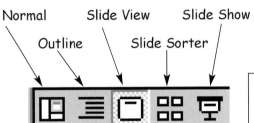

Slide View is only used for viewing the presentation.

## To select a background colour:

Click on Format

Background

Click here for colour options.

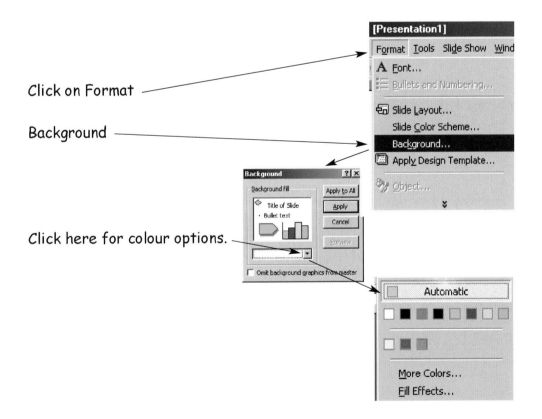

Click on a colour to highlight.

The colour chosen will then be visible in the preview box above the current colour.

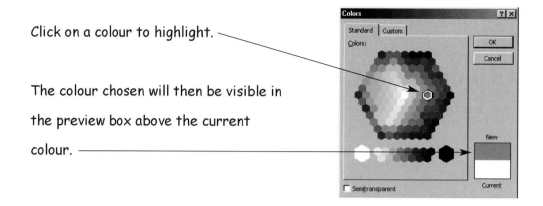

There are various options which can be explored here.

For this example two colours with horizontal shading are used.

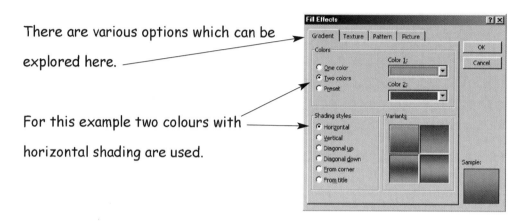

Click on Apply to All to add this background colour to all the slides created in this presentation.

Make sure this box is not ticked. Click to remove the tick.

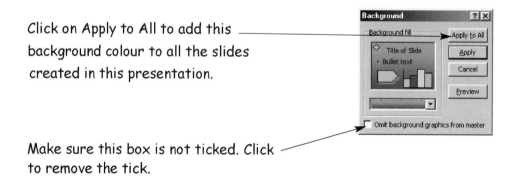

In this example WordArt is chosen for the first slide. See Chapter 11 for more details.

The WordArt Toolbar is shown below.

N.B. WordArt must be highlighted to edit.

To Colour text Click here

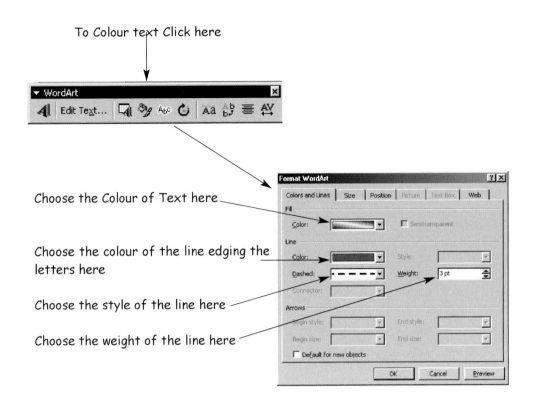

Choose the Colour of Text here

Choose the colour of the line edging the letters here

Choose the style of the line here

Choose the weight of the line here

Objects can be drawn using the Drawing Toolbar. See Chapter 6 for more details.

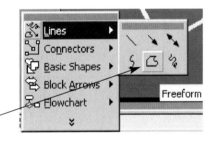

In this example Freeform is chosen from the AutoShapes menu.

To use Freeform to draw angles Click on the slide at the point where the first line is to start.

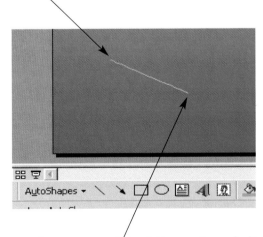

Move the cursor to the corner point of the angle and click again. Do NOT hold down the Shift key while performing this action.

Move the cursor to the final point of the line and this time double click to indicate the end of the Freeform shape.

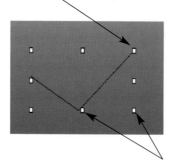

The shape will be indicated on the screen by handles at each corner and the middle of each side. This indicates the shape is highlighted and can be altered.

To change the width of the lines open the Line style menu on the Drawing Toolbar and choose the desired width.

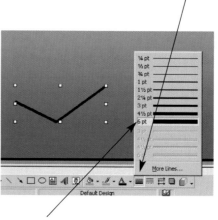

For this example 6pt was chosen.

To change the colour of the lines open the Line Colour menu on the Drawing Toolbar and choose the desired colour.

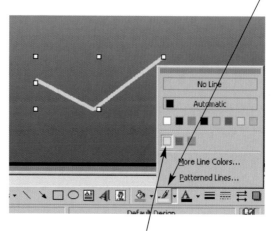

For this example yellow was chosen as a good contrast to the blue background.

Here four angles have been added to the Title screen.

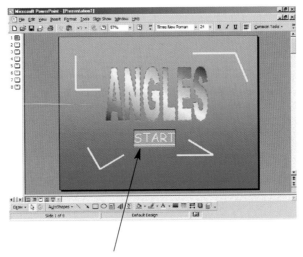

A Rectangle has been added and the word START typed. When using shapes simply start typing once the shape has been placed on the screen/page and the words will automatically appear inside the shape.

To Insert additional slides click on

Insert and New Slide

OR Click on the button on the Toolbar

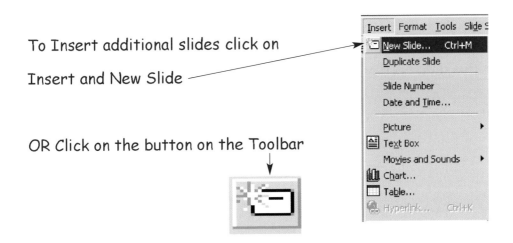

As mentioned above all text must be placed inside a Text Box unless using WordArt.

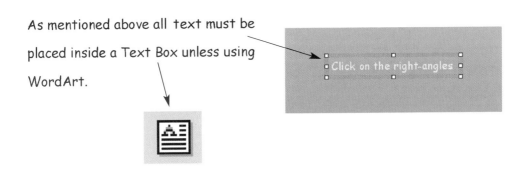

Set up the page as required.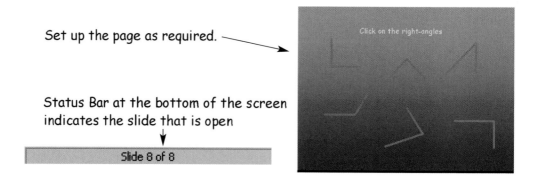

Status Bar at the bottom of the screen
indicates the slide that is open
↓

Slide 8 of 8

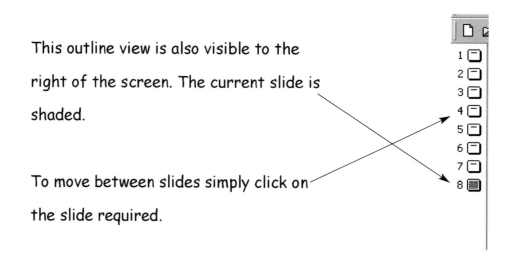

This outline view is also visible to the
right of the screen. The current slide is
shaded.

To move between slides simply click on
the slide required.

In this example an answer page is
created for each of the angles.

It is important to create as many of the
slides as possible before adding
hyperlinks.

## Adding hyperlinks:

A hyperlink is simply the means by which one slide is linked to another. This can be done with the whole slide or a specific object. In this example it is important to use an object so the children can move between slides.

Highlight the object to be linked. In this case the top left-hand angle on Slide Two.

Click on Insert on the Toolbar and then Hyperlink on the Drop-down menu that appears.

Hyperlinks can be created to web pages, but for this example click on:
Place in This Document

Click on the Slide to be linked.

In this example it is Slide Three.

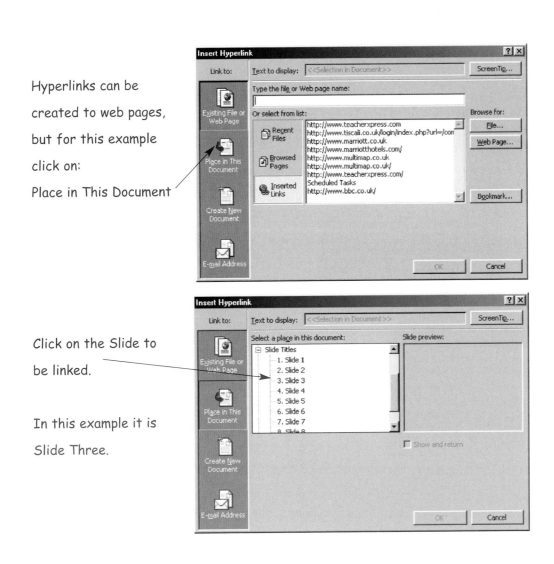

A preview of the Slide will appear.

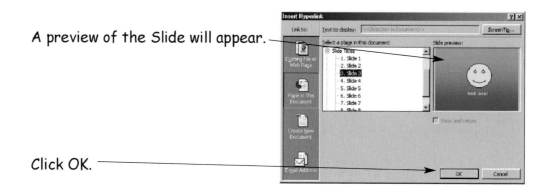

Click OK.

Hyperlinks are set up from each angle to an answer slide.

A Hyperlink is set up from the word END to the Title slide.

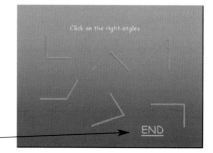

Hyperlinks are also set up from the START button on the Title slide and from an arrow or BACK button on each answer slide.

Hyperlinks do not work in any other than the Slide Show option.

To view the Slide Show make sure the current Slide is Slide 1. Click on Slide view on the Toolbar. Click on each angle and the START and END buttons to check the Hyperlinks are in the correct position.

## Adding animation:

Animation and sound effects can also be added to objects within a Slide.

Right mouse button click on the object.

Choose Custom Animation from the menu that appears.

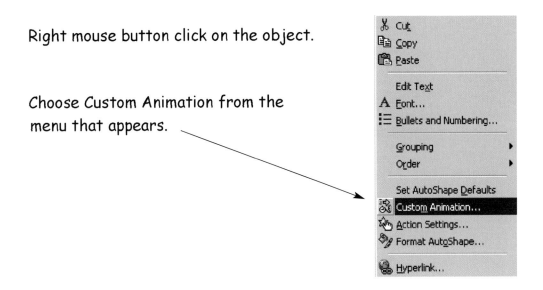

Choose the object to be animated. More than one object can be chosen with different effects for each.

Click here to preview the effect chosen.

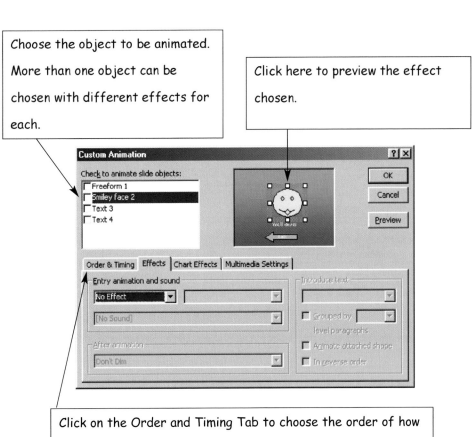

Click on the Order and Timing Tab to choose the order of how each object is to be animated.

Any objects that are not chosen will automatically appear on the Slide when it first opens.

## Order and timing:

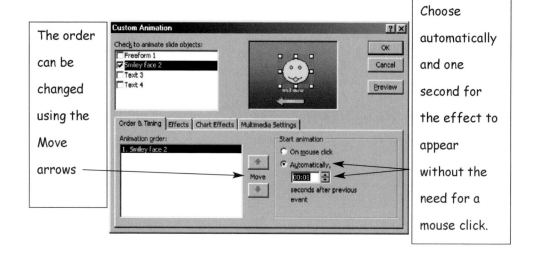

The order can be changed using the Move arrows

Choose automatically and one second for the effect to appear without the need for a mouse click.

## Effects:

Click on the object to be animated.

Click to Preview.

Choose effect for entry of object here.

Choose sound for object here.

Choose an effect to finish. 'Don't Dim' leaves the object unaltered.

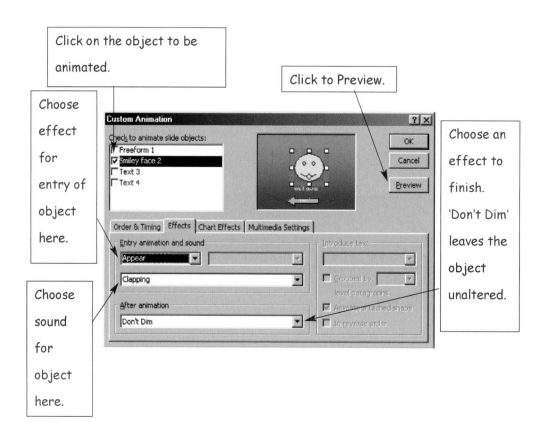

## Suggestions:

Interactive presentations can be used for:

- Interactive books
- Adventures where a number of options are given on each slide
- Science experiments
- Geography – e.g. a explanation on rainfall
- History – e.g. the Tudors either as an information exercise or assessment where children have to write answers on a paper worksheet.
- Numeracy – introducing a new topic or for the mental maths section. The timing could be set so children work through the presentation independently.

# CHAPTER 9

# Making games: tables

Tables are very useful for making games to be used as tabletop activities:

Click Table,

Insert and

Table

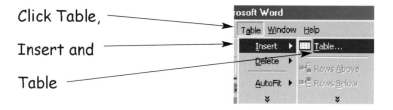

This option allows for choice of number of columns and rows:

AutoFit allows for a variety of options which suit different purposes.

AutoFormat provides a choice of table formats.

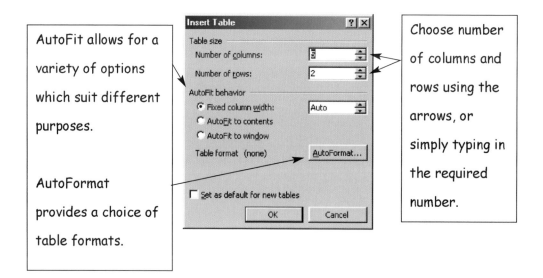

Choose number of columns and rows using the arrows, or simply typing in the required number.

OR click one of the Table buttons on the Standard Toolbar:

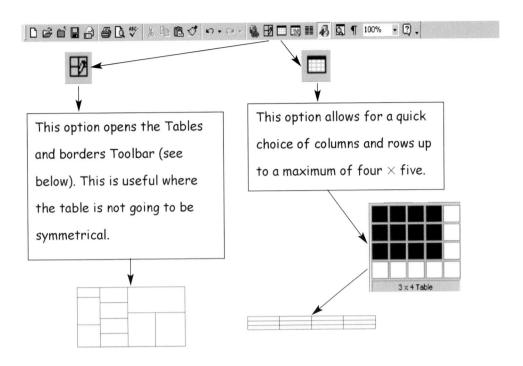

This option opens the Tables and borders Toolbar (see below). This is useful where the table is not going to be symmetrical.

This option allows for a quick choice of columns and rows up to a maximum of four × five.

3 x 4 Table

## Tables and Borders Toolbar

Only the main options have been shown here.

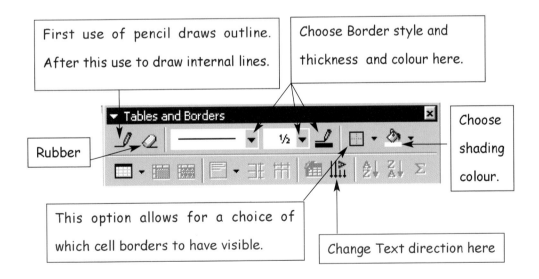

First use of pencil draws outline. After this use to draw internal lines.

Choose Border style and thickness and colour here.

Rubber

Choose shading colour.

This option allows for a choice of which cell borders to have visible.

Change Text direction here

**These examples show games made with tables:**

Card game:

Card game – this illustration shows two pages from a set of cards.

This card game was made using a table three × three. The column width was altered using the tables menu.

For the reverse of the cards:

With the curser in the top left-hand cell of the table Click on Table on the Toolbar

Click on Table Properties

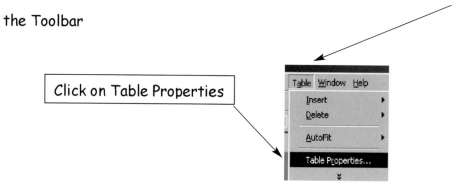

In Row choose 5 cm for the first and third rows, and 1 cm for the middle row. Choose the Row height option as 'exactly'.

In Column choose 5 cm as the preferred width for Columns one and three, and 1 cm for Column two.

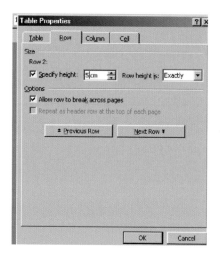

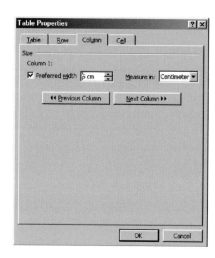

Place the curser in cell 2, click to highlight and click on Format and
Borders and Shading:

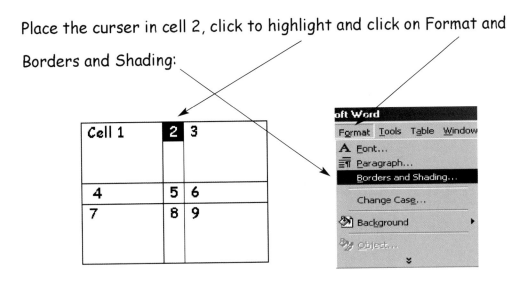

Use the buttons in
this section to delete
the lines at the top
and bottom of cell
two.
Repeat process for
cell eight.

For cells four and six
delete the left and right
hand borders.

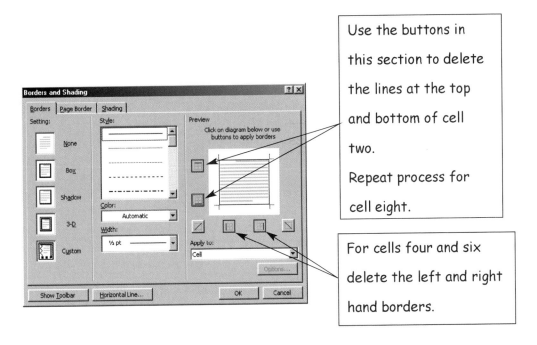

For the picture side of the cards delete all the borders.

The pictures were created using AutoShapes for this illustration. ClipArt allows for a variety of pictures appropriate to the purpose of the game. The pictures need to be placed in the middle of the cell.

For the back of the cards click on the Shading Tab in the Borders and Shading menu.

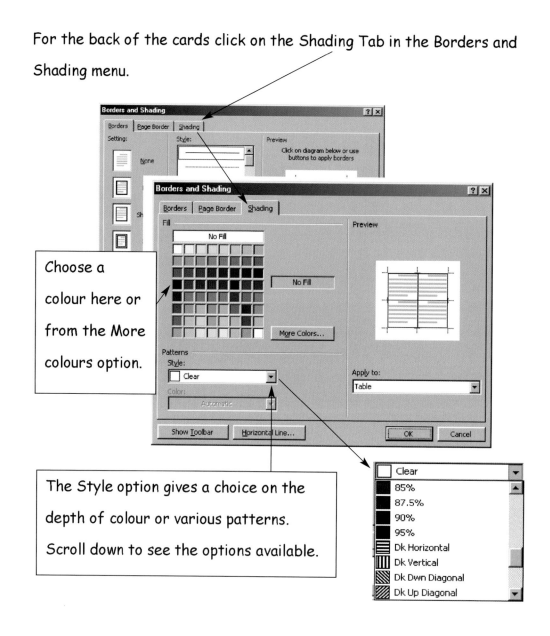

Choose a colour here or from the More colours option.

The Style option gives a choice on the depth of colour or various patterns. Scroll down to see the options available.

Printed on card and laminated the playing cards are cut out using the reverse side of the cards as a guide.

Suggested packs of cards could include:

> Numbers
> Times tables
> Initial phonics
> Rhyming words
> Words and pictures match

Teddy Bear's quilt:

This example is made using a table drawn using the Tables and Borders Toolbar. This allows for the single row at the top of the table for the pillow, and the lower section as the squares of the quilt.

Matching playing cards show only the quilt patterns. Children can place these individually or play together to see who completes their quilt first.

Subtle differences in shape colour and number of shapes makes the game more complicated.

Sentence cards:

Colour coded cards can be made for sentence formation. The example here is for use in the early years, but could be adapted for use with a variety of words. Prefixes and Suffixes could be incorporated into a similar exercise.

| The cat | The dog |
|---------|---------|
| Mum | I |

| am going | ran |
|----------|-----|
| is going | can go |
| can look | can run |
| went | can get |

| Dad | The rat |
|-----|---------|
| The man | The hen |

| can look | like |
|----------|------|
| can play | can hop |
| looks | runs |
| hops | is |

| in the bin. | up the tree. |
|-------------|--------------|
| in the sky. | at the dog. |
| in the box. | to the shop. |
| on the bed. | to the van. |
| in the park. | at the cat. |
| to school. | on a log. |

Choose the colour option in the Borders and Shading menu.

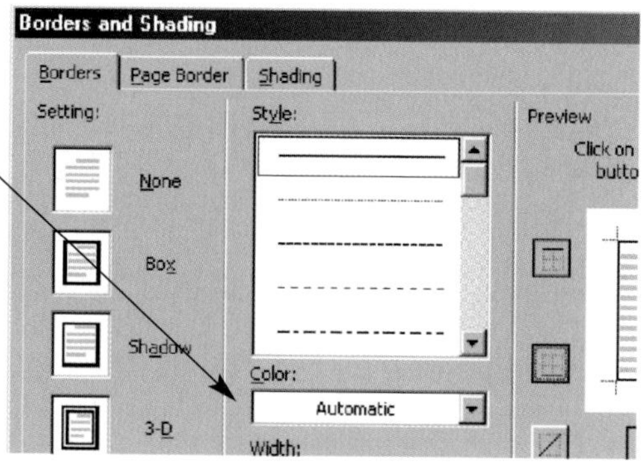

**Borders and Shading**

Borders | Page Border | Shading

Setting:

None

Box

Shadow

3-D

Style:

Color:

Automatic

Width:

Preview

Click on
butto

The colour of the border indicates the position of the word in the sentence: green, orange and red, as in traffic lights.

# Writing frames: backgrounds and borders

For presenting writing it is simple to create borders and backgrounds which can either be printed out for writing by hand, or used in the computer to produce a piece of work ready for mounting and display.

## Backgrounds

With a new document, insert a picture from ClipArt and drag to the largest size possible to fill the page.

The margins can be altered to make the picture fill the whole page in File, Page Setup:

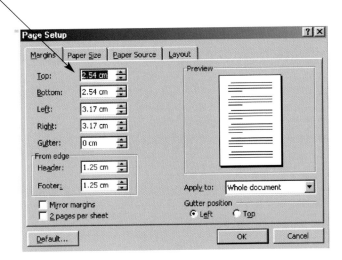

Alternatively, click and drag on the rulers at either side of the screen. This can be awkward, depending on the percentage of zoom: 100 per cent is easier than 50 per cent.

Right mouse click on the picture and open the Picture Toolbar.

The two options used here are Image Control and Text Wrapping.

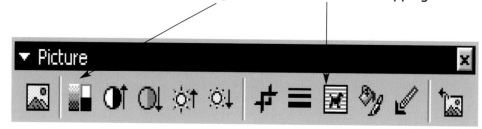

In the Text

Wrapping option

choose Behind

Text.

- Square
- Tight
- Behind Text
- In Front of Text
- Top and Bottom
- Through
- Edit Wrap Points

In the Format

Object option

choose Watermark

for a pale

background

- Automatic
- Grayscale
- Black & White
- ✓ Watermark

Children can type directly onto the background and the printed result is ready for display. Older children can experiment with their own backgrounds.

If children click on the picture they may alter the order of picture to text. For younger children the paper can be printed with the Watermark first, then replaced in the printer for the text.

The Lion

Older children can also experiment with using WordArt for writing text as the Watermark will automatically show through between the letters. This does not work with a Text Box, although other Text Wrapping options will produce a variety of interesting results.

## Borders:

An example of how to create these is shown with the posters in Chapter 11.

Page borders can be entered using the Borders and Shading menu found under Format.

Choose the Page Border option.

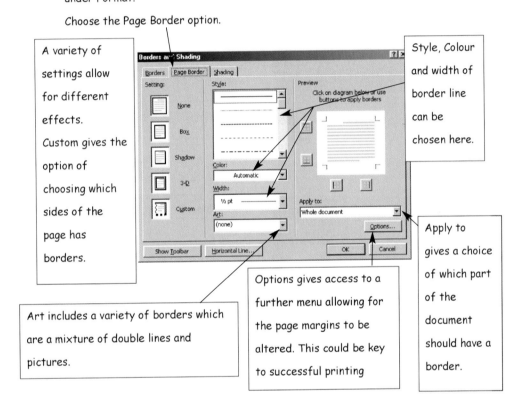

A variety of settings allow for different effects.
Custom gives the option of choosing which sides of the page has borders.

Style, Colour and width of border line can be chosen here.

Art includes a variety of borders which are a mixture of double lines and pictures.

Options gives access to a further menu allowing for the page margins to be altered. This could be key to successful printing

Apply to gives a choice of which part of the document should have a border.

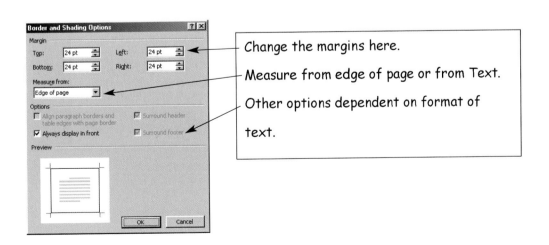

Change the margins here.

Measure from edge of page or from Text.

Other options dependent on format of text.

## BorderArt in Publisher

Windows Office Applications are changing all the time and a feature in one aspect, say Word, is becoming part of another e.g. Publisher. However, in Windows 2000, Publisher allows for the creation of BorderArt from any ClipArt or picture image. Text can be typed in the same way as in Word. The only difference with Publisher is that all text has to be typed into a text box.

Open a blank publication in Publisher:

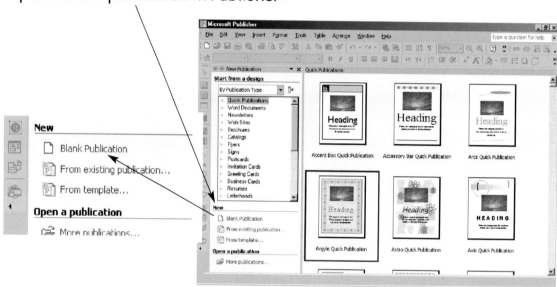

Click on Text Box button and then click on page and drag to size.

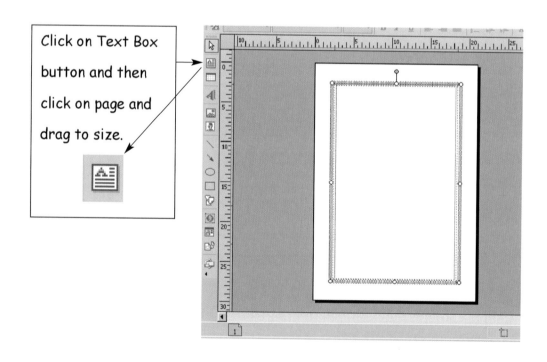

In the Format menu choose

Text Box.

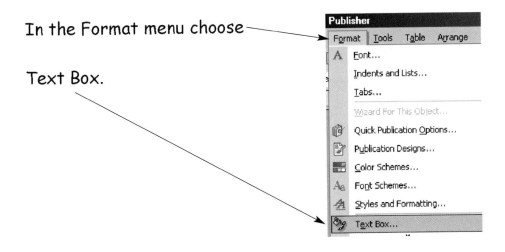

In the Colours and Lines option

Click on BorderArt.

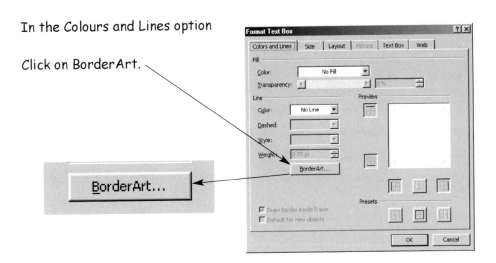

Scroll to see available borders. Custom borders
are added to this menu.

A preview of
the border is
shown here.

Click on

Create

Custom

to make

new

border

options.

In this menu

the apples

have been

stretched to

fit the

border.

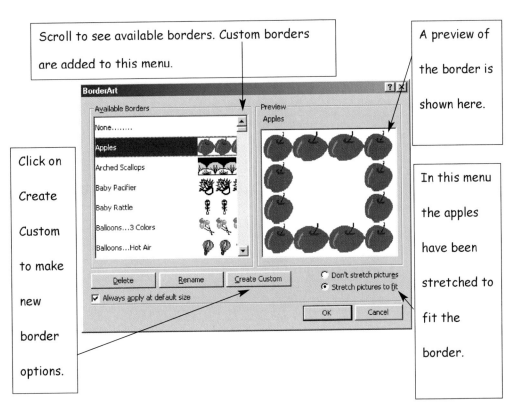

69

Click on Select Picture

This option links to ClipArt –

Click to remove the tick if the

picture is located elsewhere.

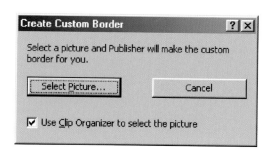

Type in a keyword to locate picture

e.g. cat

Click OK to create the border

Import provides another

opportunity to use a picture

located elsewhere on the

computer.

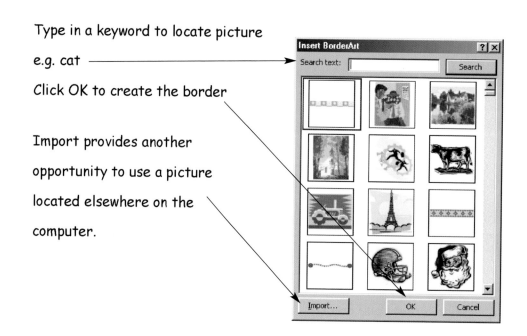

Enter a name for the new border

Click OK to insert the
border.

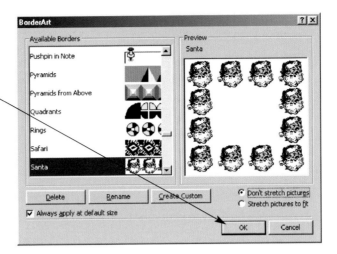

This final menu gives options
for altering the weight of the
line and which sides of the
Text Box should have borders.

The Colour and Transparency
options place a background
colour in the Text Box at the
chosen transparency density.

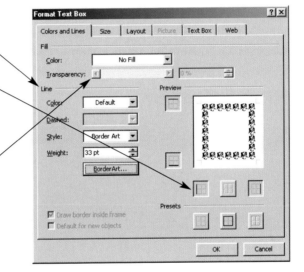

No Fill Colour

Fill colour purple; Transparency 56 per cent

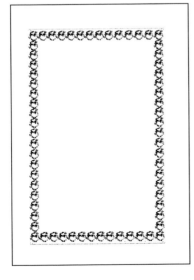

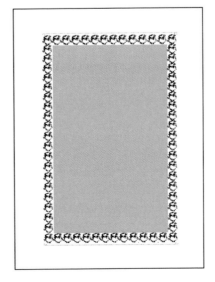

# Creating posters using WordArt and AutoShapes

Posters can easily be created on the computer. If the Publisher application is used, there are a variety of templates which can be adapted to suit individual needs. Publisher also allows for larger posters, although this involves cutting and pasting the paper to fit. Here the posters were created in Word on A4 paper.

## Using an A3 printer

If an A3 printer is

available then click

on

File

Print

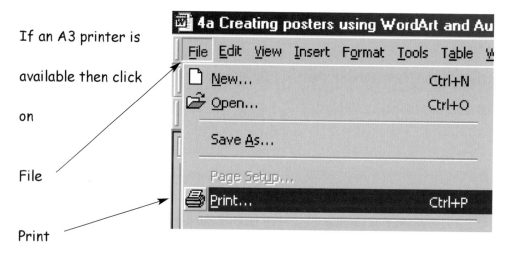

Choose the correct printer here

Click on Scale to Paper Size at the bottom right hand corner of the pop-up menu.

Choose A3 paper from the menu. Then Click OK.

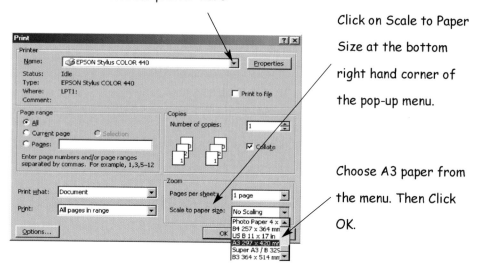

## Creating Posters

The posters illustrated in Chapter 1 were created as shown below: For instructions on creating text boxes see Chapter 4.

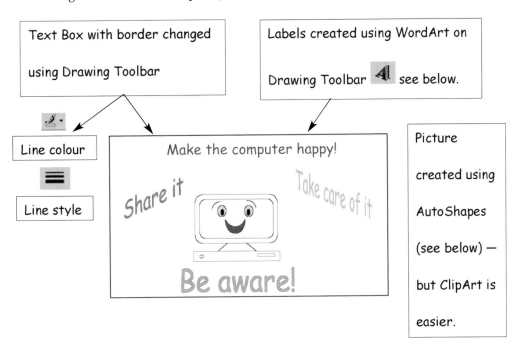

Text Box with border changed using Drawing Toolbar

Labels created using WordArt on Drawing Toolbar — see below.

Line colour

Line style

Make the computer happy!

Share it

Take care of it

Be aware!

Picture created using AutoShapes (see below) — but ClipArt is easier.

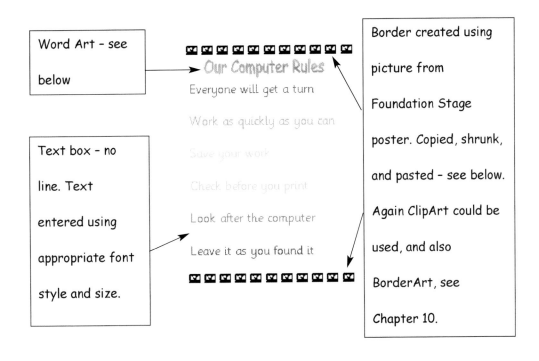

Word Art – see below

Text box – no line. Text entered using appropriate font style and size.

Our Computer Rules

Everyone will get a turn

Work as quickly as you can

Save your work

Check before you print

Look after the computer

Leave it as you found it

Border created using picture from Foundation Stage poster. Copied, shrunk, and pasted – see below. Again ClipArt could be used, and also BorderArt, see Chapter 10.

**WordArt:**

Click on WordArt Button on Drawing Toolbar

WordArt Gallery

Choose a style and colour and click OK. This can be edited at any point. For the posters this style was chosen.

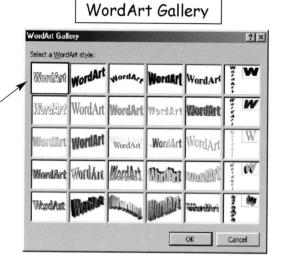

Choose font size here.

Choose font style here.

For Bold or Italic click here.

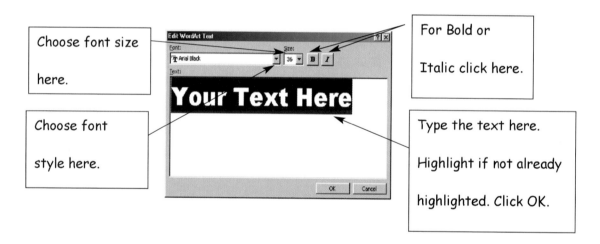

Type the text here. Highlight if not already highlighted. Click OK.

To edit click on the WordArt (right mouse button)

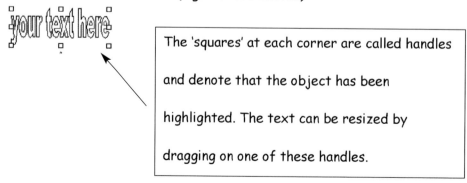

The 'squares' at each corner are called handles and denote that the object has been highlighted. The text can be resized by dragging on one of these handles.

The following menu will appear.

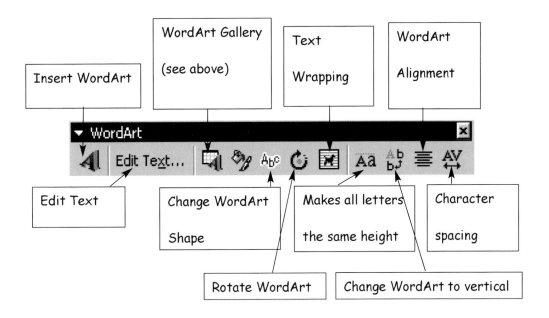

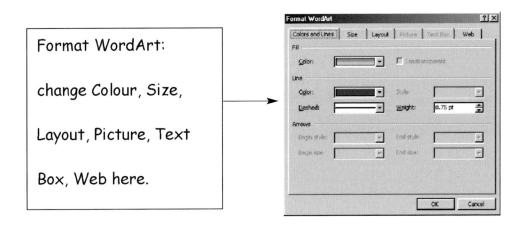

## AutoShapes

Locate on the Draw Toolbar

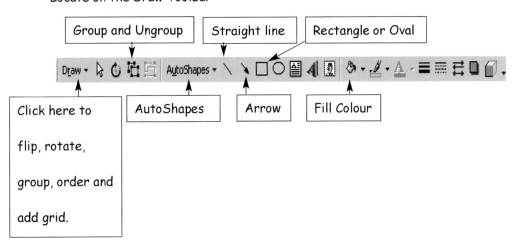

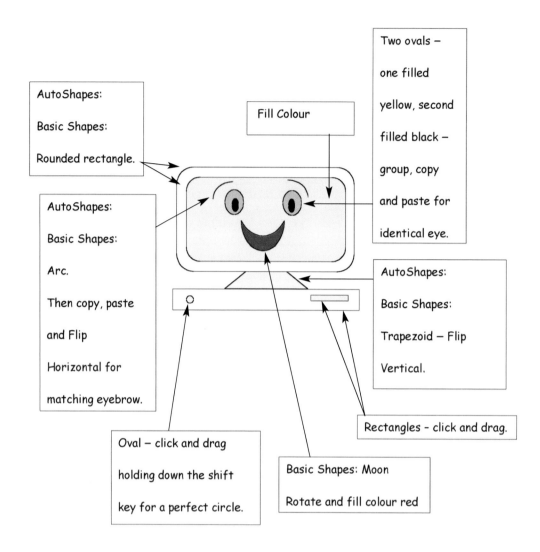

AutoShapes:

Basic Shapes:

Rounded rectangle.

Fill Colour

Two ovals –
one filled
yellow, second
filled black –
group, copy
and paste for
identical eye.

AutoShapes:

Basic Shapes:

Arc.

Then copy, paste

and Flip

Horizontal for

matching eyebrow.

AutoShapes:

Basic Shapes:

Trapezoid – Flip

Vertical.

Rectangles – click and drag.

Oval – click and drag

holding down the shift

key for a perfect circle.

Basic Shapes: Moon

Rotate and fill colour red

To make into one picture, hold down the shift key and click on each component of the picture. Then, when all are highlighted by handles, click on group button on Draw Toolbar.

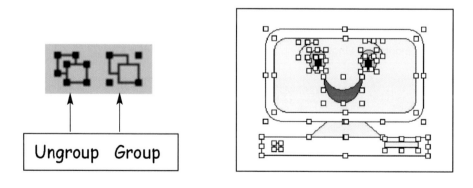

Ungroup  Group

## To create a row of pictures for a border:

Copy the picture and reduce in size (Click on one of the handles in another corner of the picture and drag towards the centre until the picture is the size you want). Do not place inside a Text Box.

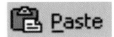

Objects must be highlighted to copy

Copy this smaller image. Place the cursor where the first picture is to be placed. Simply press Paste and then drag each new image into place, until the required number is reached. These images can be placed as close to each other as required.

Click on each image in turn, while holding down the Shift key and group the images together. In order to line them up a line can be drawn using AutoShapes.

Once the row is complete, delete the line, and then group the objects together as above.

This line of images can now be copied and pasted to form a row at the bottom of the page. Alternatively it can be flipped and rotated to form borders at each edge of the page. The size can be altered by stretching the image.

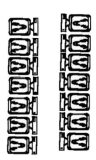

# Using the Internet

# The Internet: searching, copying and pasting

This is not an easy task, and can be frustrating due the wealth of available information and the sheer volume of 'hits' when searching for something.

Without criticising any search engines, children always seem to be very confident about which are the 'best' search engines, and then often can't find the information they are looking for. If they do find the information they may find it difficult to actually read it and locate the relevant points. These are sophisticated skills and children need to be taught to use search engines effectively, but also be restricted in their searches.

The same is true of adults, who are often frustrated by not being able to find exactly what they wanted. So where to start?

1. Look for websites which have already done some of the legwork. These are sites that have collated a variety of education sites together and sorted them into various categories. Two such sites are:

   > www.teacherxpress.com
   > www.sfe.co.uk (learning resources – linkbank)

2. Check out sites for teachers and follow through the links they have put on their web pages.

   > www.primaryresources.co.uk
   > www.sitesforteachers.com
   > www.bbc.co.uk/learning
   > www.teachingideas.co.uk
   > www.schools-resources.co.uk

3. Use a search engine that is easy to use and reliable – one that gives a good number of 'hits' but without too many that are purely sales!

4. Make sure the search engine has advanced features such as looking for a phrase, e.g. 'Little Red Riding Hood'. It will only locate those sites which have this phrase in that order. Even though this may still locate online shopping, it is a start in the right direction.

5. Check that the search engine provides enough information underneath each 'hit' so that it is possible to sift through them quickly and find the ones with the most useful information. Only check out those sites that look as if they will be interesting.

6. Choose the words carefully when searching. Use either a '+' sign or ',' to refine your search e.g. Michelangelo, Sistine Chapel or Michelangelo + Sistine Chapel. Don't just type a single word but add extra information to reduce the number of hits.

7. Limit the time spent searching the Internet – time is valuable and it is very easy to be put off if locating the information takes too long. A limit of about 15 minutes per search is a good idea. It is important not to get distracted by other potentially interesting sites which are not directly related to the target information. Save these sites in the appropriate folder and check them out another time.

8. Bookmark favourite and most useful sites. Organise the favourites or bookmarked list so that locating these sites on future occasions is easy. Label the folders with curriculum areas, and place them all in a master folder with the class name. If the school is networked, then set up a series of folders that everyone can access. In this instance, sorting them into key stages might be a more suitable arrangement – even if some sites are saved in more than one folder.

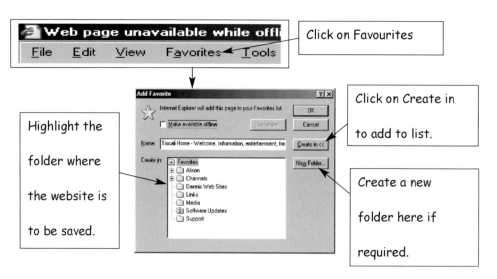

## To organise your favourites:

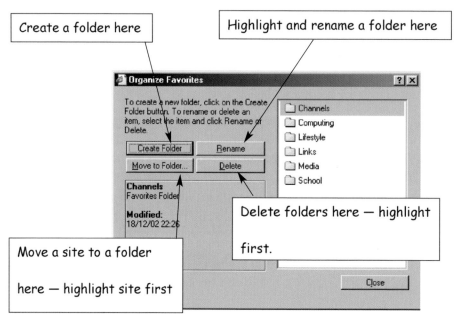

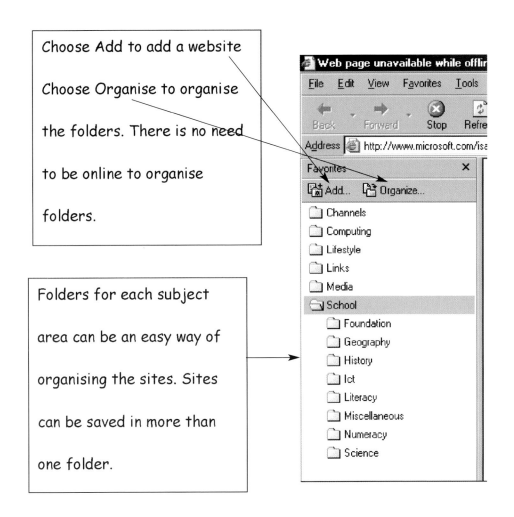

Choose Add to add a website

Choose Organise to organise the folders. There is no need to be online to organise folders.

Folders for each subject area can be an easy way of organising the sites. Sites can be saved in more than one folder.

## Copying and pasting from the Internet

It isn't always possible to copy from the Internet and, as technology develops, some sites are well protected. However, there are many sites with worksheets and other resources for school which can be downloaded or copied. Sometimes it is enough just to print off the page – but the page break may be in the wrong position, or there is extra unwanted material. Make sure to include the web page address so as not to infringe copyright.

Open a Word document before opening the Internet – the link with Word should be visible on the Status Bar.

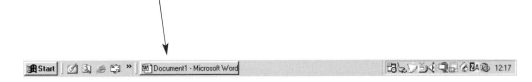

### Copying text:

Highlight the text to be copied – in some instance the pictures will be included in this.

### Click with the right mouse button for the Drop-down menu.

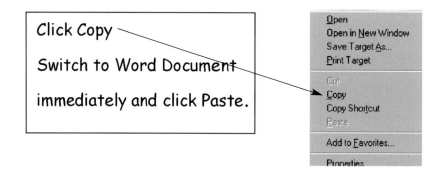

Click Copy

Switch to Word Document immediately and click Paste.

Once pasted, the text can be altered to suit: change the font size, style, edit the text etc.

It is only possible to copy one piece of text at a time. It must be pasted into a document before copying anything else.

### Copying pictures:

Click on the picture with the right mouse button.

### The Drop-down menu will appear.

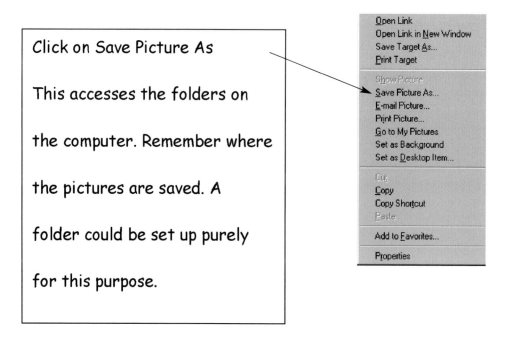

Click on Save Picture As

This accesses the folders on

the computer. Remember where

the pictures are saved. A

folder could be set up purely

for this purpose.

Multiple pictures can be saved without having to paste these into the final document until everything has been found. This is because the pictures are saved into a folder, whilst text is simply copied.

**To Insert the picture:**

Click on Insert

Click on Picture

Click on From File

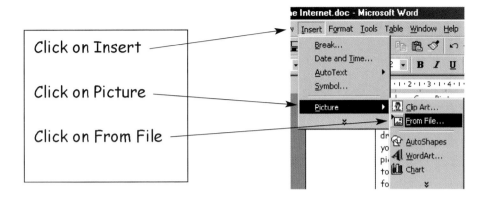

Locate the folder where
the picture was saved.

Locate the picture

Click to highlight and click
on Insert.

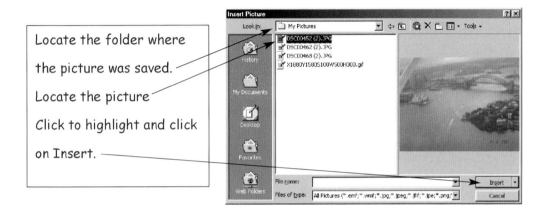

The picture can be altered using the picture format toolbar. See Chapter 4 for more
details.

# The Internet: software downloads and locating files and folders

Companies are beginning to paste extra support on their websites. This can be useful for:

- Accessing support, help sheets and upgrades
- Accessing extra activities

If software is unfamiliar, it is worth typing its name into a reliable search engine.

There are several help sheets and tutorials available online to support the use of applications like Word, Excel, PowerPoint etc. Type the name of the application plus:

- Help
- Tutorials
- Activities

If this produces too many hits then make sure the hits are all English, and maybe even restrict the search to the UK. Good search engines have this feature.

Some software companies have extra resources, ideas and activities on their websites. In other cases, schools and teachers have pasted their own ideas on the Internet. These are often freely available for download.

Type the name of the program into a search engine. Extra words that may help are:

- Activities
- Help
- Support

Read the instructions on the website for downloading any extra activities.

Locate the program files on the computer and place any downloads into the appropriate files.

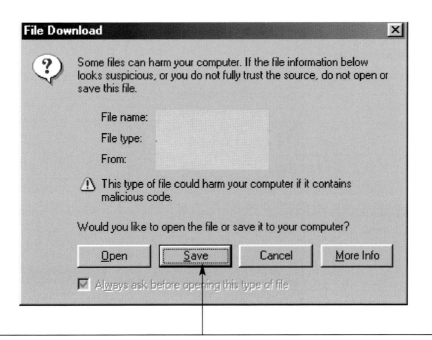

Click on Save to download the file onto your computer

Click here to locate the file – or floppy drive or CD drive if to be stored on disc/CD.

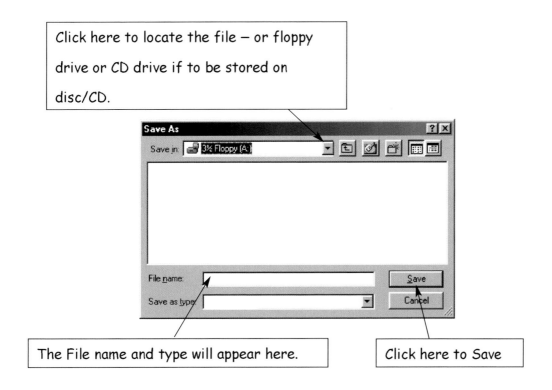

The File name and type will appear here.

Click here to Save

A dialogue box will appear and provide information on the time it will take to download and when the process is complete.

## Locating files and folders

To locate a file:

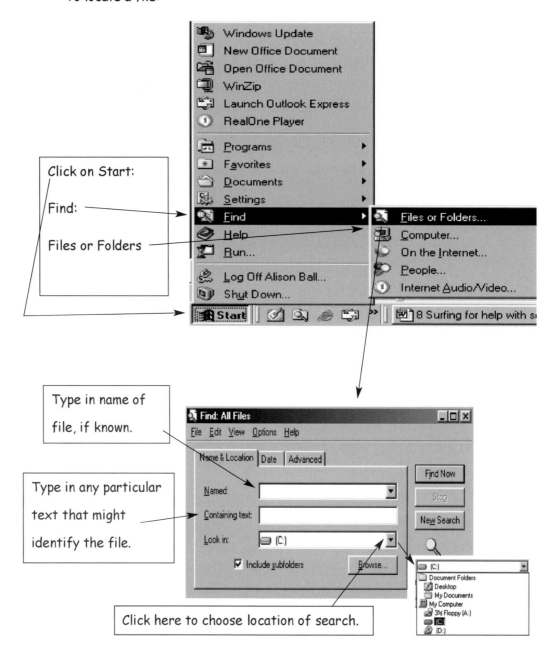

Click on Start:

Find:

Files or Folders

Type in name of file, if known.

Type in any particular text that might identify the file.

Click here to choose location of search.

Windows Explorer is another useful tool for locating files and folders, moving them around, and deleting unnecessary work. This is explained fully in Chapter Seventeen.

## School websites:

More and more teachers are making use of the Internet, and schools are developing their own websites, several of which have valuable material and resources. Obviously these change all the time. Current websites include:

> www.webschool.org.uk (North Chadderton School)
> www.emu.org.uk/numeracy/ (Sandwell Numeracy site)
> www.ambleside.digitalbrain.com (Ambleside school)
> www.snaithprimary.eril.net
> www.hitchams.suffolk.sch.uk
> www.groveroad.herts.sch.uk

Some activities are for use online, others for downloading, and others for printing off and using as worksheets.

# Auditing and organising the computer

# Auditing the computer: how to locate and load software

This chapter looks at what is already available on the computer. This can be separated into two main categories:

- Applications software: These are programs that are used to complete a variety of tasks. Examples include: word processing, database and presentation tools. Applications have to be installed in the computer.
- Software programs: These are programs which may perform several tasks but are subject or task specific, e.g. spelling adventure, touch typing course, curriculum area support, etc. These programs can be installed on the computer, but can also be used from the CD or Floppy disc. Some may only be used if the floppy or CD ROM is in the computer.

Computers often arrive with applications already loaded. Schools and LEAs add their own licensed software. It is important to know what is on the computer and how this matches the curriculum.

Even if the information is to hand, it is worth making regular checks to ensure access is easy and efficient for the children in the class. This may well change from year to year, and during the course of the year as their ICT skills develop. Programs use space on the computer and it is important to maximise this as much as possible. To uninstall programs see below under Installing programs.

## What's on the computer?

Knowing what is on the computer allows for the following:

- Planning to include ICT across the curriculum
- Matching programs to the needs of the class
- Ensuring the computer memory is maximised
- Highlighting areas for future purchasing

To check what is currently on the computer, start with the desktop display. This appears when the computer is turned on. Some LEAs have a standard screen which might appear in the form of several other screens accessed by buttons; e.g. for numeracy, literacy, science, presentation etc.

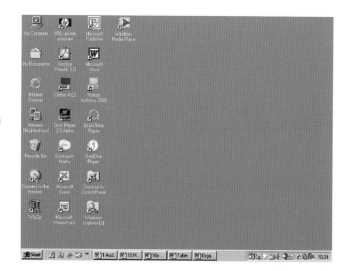

Desktop
Display

In Windows 2000 the main screen has a series of shortcuts to some of the programs.

The arrow at the bottom left-hand corner denotes

a shortcut. ────────────────────

Double click on a shortcut to access the program.

See Chapter Fifteen for information on how to set up shortcuts. Not all the applications/programs have shortcuts.

To locate these click on Start:

Click on Programs

Where an arrow appears this denotes further

options. These might include additional

information about the program.

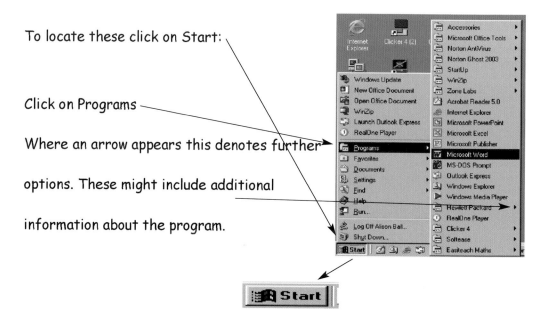

The form below can be used to record the applications and software on the computer.

| Applications | Name | Software company | Website |
|---|---|---|---|
| Word processing tools | | | |
| | | | |
| | | | |
| Database and spreadsheets | | | |
| | | | |
| Presentation | | | |
| | | | |
| Programs | Company | Website | Curriculum area |
| | | | |
| | | | |
| | | | |
| | | | |
| | | | |
| | | | |
| | | | |
| | | | |
| | | | |
| | | | |

**Word processing tools:**

There are many of these on the market aimed specifically at children. Some schools use Microsoft Word, others use alternative word processing tools designed specifically for educational use. There are arguments for and against both options.

| Using Microsoft Word | Using a word processor designed for schools |
|---|---|
| Some people argue that children should use Word from an early age as this is one of the most common word processors in current use. | Many alternatives have similar features to Word. They are simpler to use, having fewer buttons on the toolbars. |
| The toolbars in Word can be customised so that only the necessary buttons are visible (Chapter 15). | Some have separate versions for KS1 and KS2, allowing for more options as ICT skills are acquired. |
| Additional software can be purchased which reads the text as it is typed (provided there is a sound card and speakers) which is especially helpful for Foundation Stage and older SEN pupils. | Often these word processing tools have a talking facility so the children can listen to the words or sentences as they are typed. |
| Some Word Prediction tools can be used alongside Word. These predict the next word, which can then be entered using the function keys. | Word Prediction tools require some reading ability (unless they have a talk facility) and they can take a while to learn the words that are most commonly used by any one pupil. |

| Using Microsoft Word | Using a word processor designed for schools |
|---|---|
| There are word bank facilities which can be used within Word: Wordbar and WordAid2 for example. | Word bank facilities are available in many of these programs. These can encourage children to use words they would otherwise not attempt. |
| Templates can be created which children can use, rather than presenting them with a blank page for writing. | Many word processors have a variety of activities you can use, or edit, which meet the needs of the curriculum. |
| There are activities and examples of work created by schools and individuals which is available on the Internet and can be downloaded. See Chapter 13. | Companies and schools are beginning to post activities they have created on the Internet for other word processors. See Chapter 13. |

## Databases and spreadsheets

Many schools are using Excel, particularly with older children. Other educational software companies have produced database and spreadsheet programs that aim to be 'user friendly' for children. (See list on page 98 for companies producing software.)

It is worth checking to see what support material and activities are available for any of the programs. There is material for Excel available on the Internet (see Chapter 12 for more details on how to search for support material on the Internet).

www.forsyth.k12.ga.us/kadkins/spreadsheet.htm
www.internet4classrooms.com/on-line_excel.htm

are both worth exploring.

## Presentation Tools

Again there are several on the market aimed at children. Many of these are similar to PowerPoint and offer a good stepping-stone to this application.

### Thoughts to consider

When deciding which applications to use, the following should be taken into consideration

- The age of the children using the application
- The ICT skills of the children
- The appropriateness of the application

### Alternatives

To locate alternative packages, check out the following Educational software companies:

| | |
|---|---|
| Black Cat | www.blackcatsoftware.com |
| Crick | www.cricksoft.com |
| Granada | www.granadalearning.com |
| Kudlian | www.kudlian.net |
| Logotron | www.logo.com |
| Softease | www.textease.com |

Or search the Internet: see Chapter Twelve for further details.

## Other software programs

Most other software will be in the form of CD ROMs (or floppy discs), which may or may not have to be loaded in the computer to allow the program to run. It is becoming easier to load software onto a computer and personal favourites can easily be installed. In most cases this should simply mean placing the CD ROM in the CD drive and then following the instructions that appear on screen. Software companies usually provide a paper copy of the installation instructions with the program.

If there are no instructions with the CD ROM then:

Open Windows Explorer        which you will find either:

- on the main screen as a shortcut

- on the Status toolbar to the right of Start at the bottom of the Desktop display

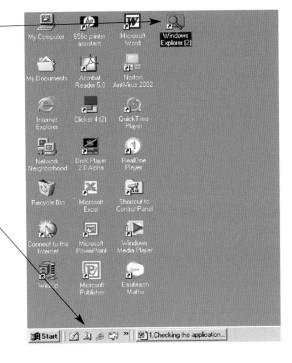

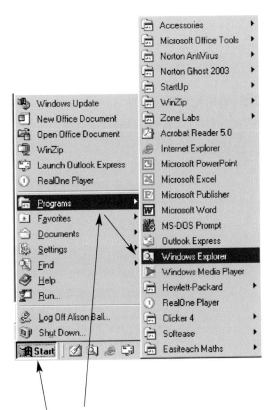

- Through Start, Programs

Choose the option for the
CD drive.

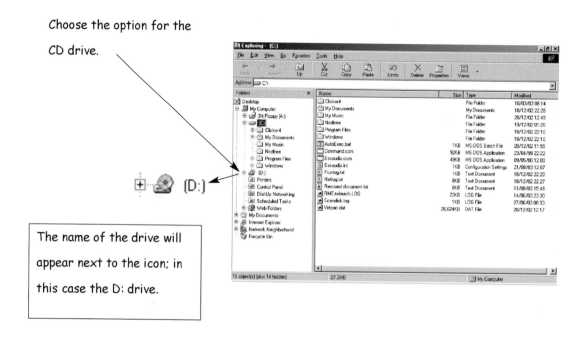

The name of the drive will
appear next to the icon; in
this case the D: drive.

Files labelled '.exe' usually contain the installation process. Click on this file to load
the software. The instructions will appear on screen.

An alternative method is found through using Start, Run.

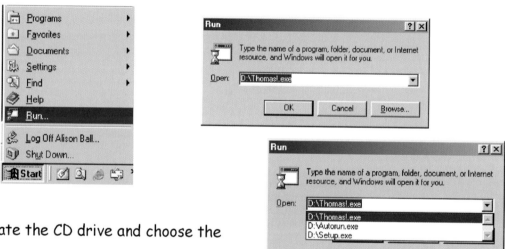

Locate the CD drive and choose the

installation option – often 'Setup.exe'

## Evaluating the contents of the classroom computer

As with many aspects of education, it is important to evaluate computer usage from
time to time. It is also essential to do this before purchasing expensive software that
may not fulfill the needs of the school.

To maximise the use of any particular application or program, the class teacher
needs to be familiar with all aspects of the software. Chapter Thirteen provides more
information on how to locate and develop this software.

Matching ICT to the needs of the class means evaluating the software to see which areas of the curriculum it covers. Use the form below as a starting point for this process. Gaps will indicate the focus for future purchasing.

Nowadays it is often possible to download demo versions of programs, these are time limited. This can be a good way of deciding if this program will fit into the curriculum. Don't download the demo until there is an opportunity to use it in lessons to give the best chance for evaluation. Where possible, the whole school could use the same demo program over the course of a couple of weeks in order to ensure that it is worth purchasing.

## Evaluating computer applications and software

| Application Curriculum area | KS | Name of program/comments |
|---|---|---|
| Word processing tools | Foundation Stage | |
| | KS1 | |
| | KS2 | |
| Database spreadsheet | Foundation Stage | |
| | KS1 | |
| | KS2 | |
| Presentation tools | Foundation Stage | |
| | KS1 | |
| | KS2 | |
| Literacy | Foundation Stage | |
| | KS1 | |
| | KS2 | |
| Numeracy | Foundation Stage | |
| | KS1 | |
| | KS2 | |
| Science | Foundation Stage | |
| | KS1 | |
| | KS2 | |

| Application Curriculum area | KS | Name of program/comments |
|---|---|---|
| DT | Foundation Stage | |
| | KS1 | |
| | KS2 | |
| Geography | Foundation Stage | |
| | KS1 | |
| | KS2 | |
| History | Foundation Stage | |
| | KS1 | |
| | KS2 | |
| PSHE | Foundation Stage | |
| | KS1 | |
| | KS2 | |
| RE | Foundation Stage | |
| | KS1 | |
| | KS2 | |
| Miscellaneous | Foundation Stage | |
| | KS1 | |
| | KS2 | |

# CHAPTER 15

# Customising the desktop display: icons and shortcuts

The desktop display can often appear cluttered. It is important, in the classroom, for access to be as quick as possible. By changing the layout of the display it can be made more accessible. Older children can be shown how to locate and open programs and files using the start menu as this is a useful skill. For younger children, quicker access is required using shortcuts if it is not possible for the program to be already opened for them.

An **icon** is the picture on the display which will allow you to access a program, with a double click of the mouse. A **shortcut** is an icon which has an arrow in the bottom left-hand corner of the icon. This is a shortcut to the application, program or file.

| An icon that is not a shortcut. Do not delete. |  |  | A shortcut icon. This can be deleted if not required. |
|---|---|---|---|

## Icons and shortcuts:

It is possible to move the icons and shortcuts around on the display – simply click with the left mouse button and drag. It may be important to move the icons around so that children are quickly directed to the program or file. By isolating an icon to one side of the screen, children will find it quickly – shortcuts to that day's work, or to specific folders that can then be located instantly.

The icons and shortcuts can be arranged alphabetically so that children get used to their location. This is helpful if all the classroom computers are set up in a similar way so the transfer from one class to another is easy.

**To arrange icons alphabetically:**

Click with the right mouse button anywhere on the

blank part of the desktop display.

This pop-up menu will appear.

Click with the left mouse button on Arrange Icons

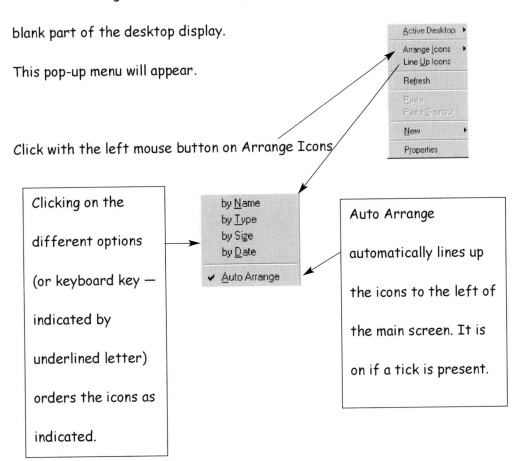

Clicking on the different options (or keyboard key — indicated by underlined letter) orders the icons as indicated.

Auto Arrange automatically lines up the icons to the left of the main screen. It is on if a tick is present.

**To isolate a specific icon:**

Click on Auto Arrange to switch off this feature – the tick will disappear. Simply click and drag by holding the left mouse button down, to move the icon to its desired location.

## To create a shortcut:

Click on Start and then Click on Programs

Locate the program/application and make sure it is highlighted, then click

on the right mouse button.

Click with the left mouse button on
Send To and the following menu will appear.

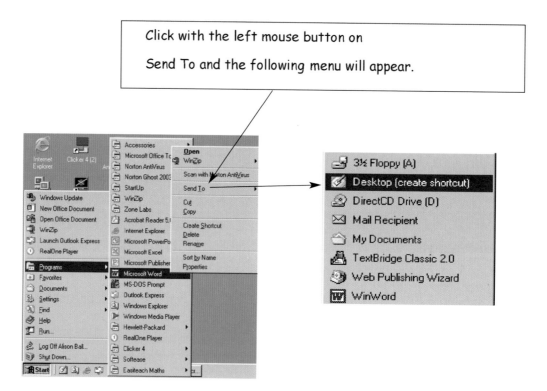

Click with the left mouse button on Desktop (Create Shortcut) and this will
automatically send a shortcut icon to the desktop display.

Click on OK with the
left mouse button to
confirm.

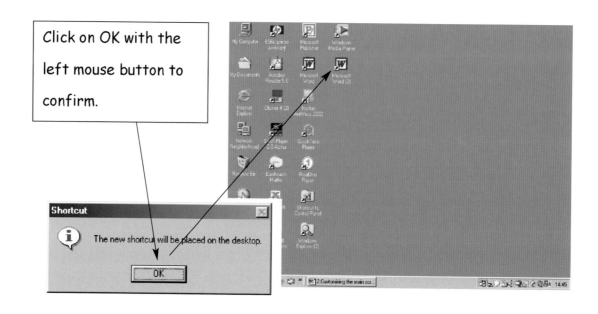

Shortcuts can be created to individual files within applications by the same method: For example – for group work a file in Word can be accessed through a shortcut.

Close the file and then click on open: (or File, Open)

Locate the file:

Click with the right mouse button on the file and the menu will appear as in the example above.

Simply follow the same procedures,

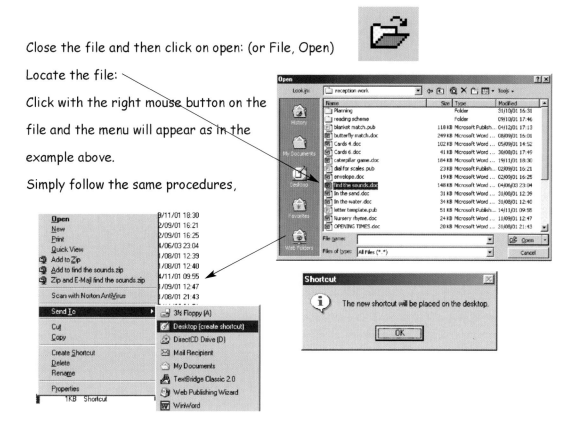

Shortcuts to folders can be created in the same way – which can be used as a first step to teaching children how to locate files on the computer, before introducing them to the Start menu.

To delete a shortcut (N.B. This will not delete the program, file or application) click on the icon with the right mouse button. The pop-up menu will appear.

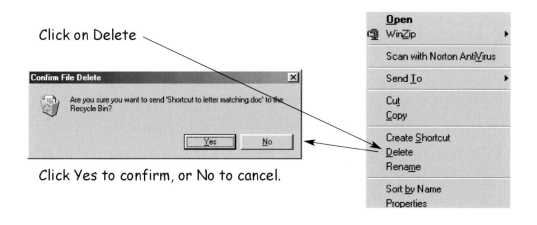

Click on Delete

Click Yes to confirm, or No to cancel.

This moves the shortcut icon to the recycle bin. It can be retrieved from here if a mistake has been made by a double click on the recycle bin icon. Then click and drag on the item to be restored to the desktop display.

This recycle bin is empty

Papers indicate items in the bin

# Maintenance

# CHAPTER 16

# Maintenance: the outside of the computer and backup procedure

It is important to look after the computer – and that includes the outside of the machine as well as the inside. There is no need to physically open the machine as there are several operations which, if performed on a regular basis, will extend the life of the computer.

## Outside:

- It is important to keep the computer as clean as possible. Guards for the keyboard and screen are useful and help to keep the dust away. Try not to pile things up around the computer.

- If the keys get sticky or dirty because of use, wipe them with a damp cloth. It is possible to purchase keyboard gloves, which will protect the keyboard. See Chapter 3 for more information on alternative keyboards.

- The screen on the monitor is best not touched (in fact, on laptops it can damage the screen) but they should be regularly dusted and wiped, if necessary, with a soft damp cloth. Cleaning tools can be purchased from computer shops if required.

- Food and drink should be kept away from the computer. If, for any reason, there is a spillage on the keyboard, switch off the computer, turn the keyboard upside down and try to get as much of the liquid out as possible. Kitchen towels can be useful in this instance.

- Make sure the surface area around the computer is kept clean and dust-free as well.

- Keep all floppy discs and CD ROMs in their covers and in a box – don't build up a pile by the computer, and certainly not on the computer as this can damage the disc.

- Ensure children know how to handle floppy discs and CD ROMs properly. Use digital cameras and take photos of the children doing this, and display these by the computer. Children are more likely to respond to photos of their classmates, so these will need to be changed regularly.

## Inside the computer:

Everyone has experienced computers crashing! Much work has been lost this way.

Keep backups of all computer files. This is especially important with planning and files that are to be used again. If the computer crashes or someone reloads the software as part of routine outside maintenance, there will still be a record of all the work. If the system is networked, check to make sure a backup is taken; though a copy of important files is still worth saving on disc.

Make sure a backup is taken on a regular basis – ideally once a week if the computer is used regularly to store information. Year 6 children could be trained to perform this as a lunchtime duty. Remember this is important if the computer is free-standing and not networked.

## To set up a backup disc:

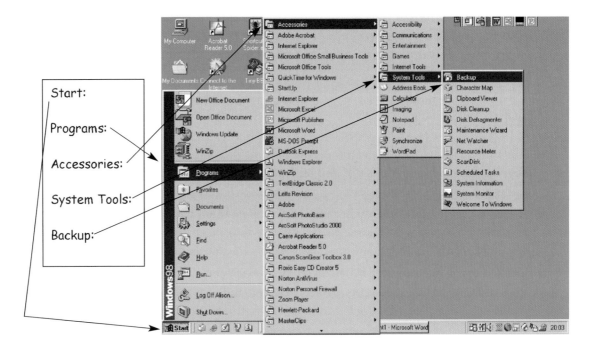

Follow through the instructions that appear:

### 2. Create a new backup job

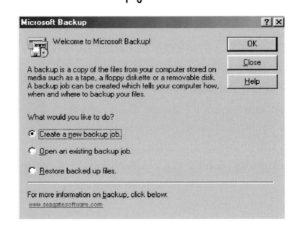

## 2. Back up My Computer

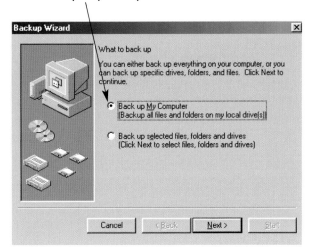

## 3. What to back up

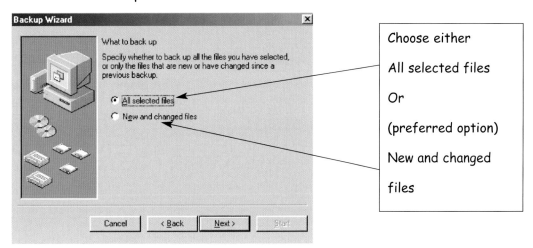

Choose either

All selected files

Or

(preferred option)

New and changed

files

## 4. Where to back up

Choose either

All selected files

Or

(preferred option)

New and changed files

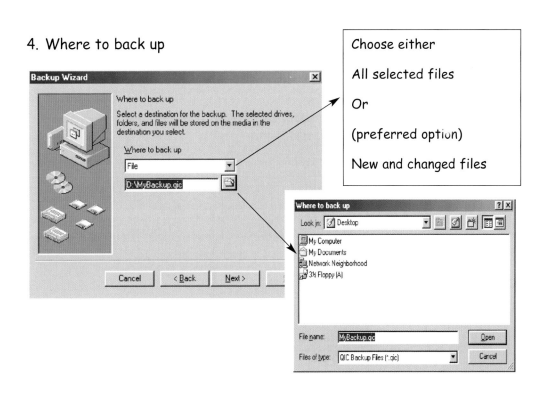

## 5. How to back up

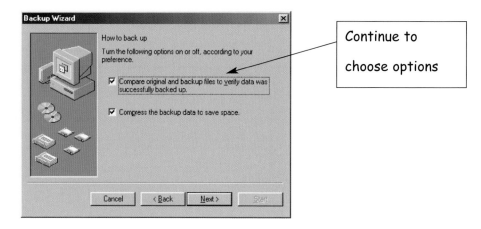

Continue to choose options

## 6. Name the back up job

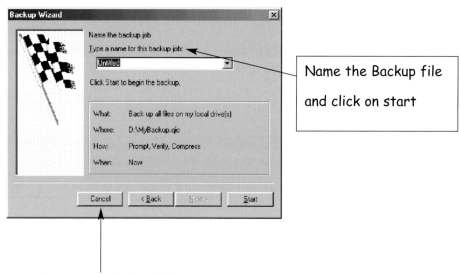

Name the Backup file and click on start

If Cancel is clicked the following menu with options will appear:

Other options

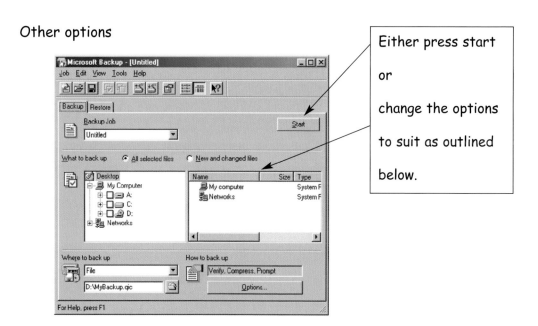

Either press start

or

change the options to suit as outlined below.

**General Tab:**

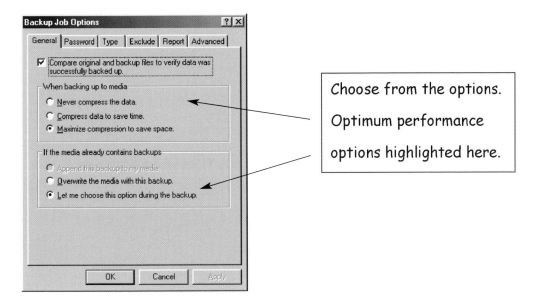

Choose from the options.
Optimum performance
options highlighted here.

**Password Tab:**

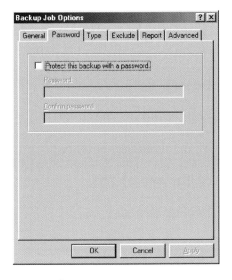

Option available to
password protect the
Backup file.

**Type Tab:**

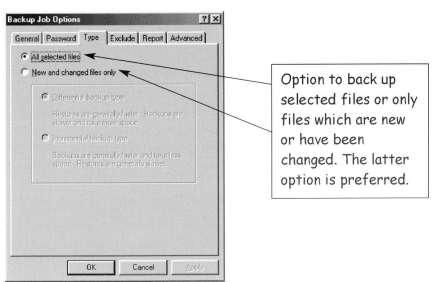

Option to back up
selected files or only
files which are new
or have been
changed. The latter
option is preferred.

## Exclude Tab:

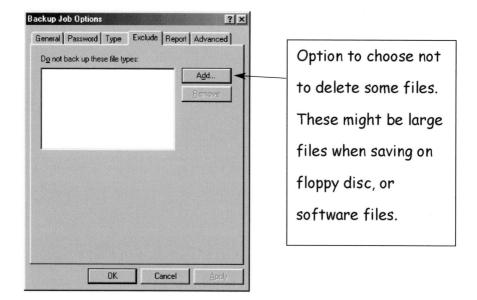

Option to choose not to delete some files. These might be large files when saving on floppy disc, or software files.

## Report Tab:

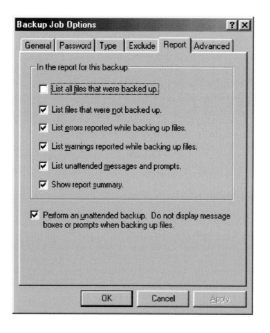

Several options available depending on the level of information required at the end of the Backup process.

(For the purpose of this book the Advanced Tab is not included.)

Once set up, the Backup will perform the same actions every time it is used. This means that on future occasions it will not take as long to complete.

If the 'Back up new and changed files' options has been chosen as part of the file, then the time taken to back up will be minimal.

**To start the Backup:**

Open Backup as above: Programs: Accessories: System Tools: Backup

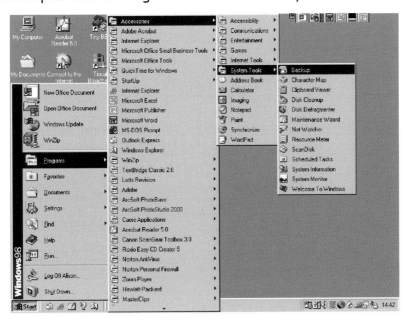

The following menu will appear:

Click on:

Open an existing backup job

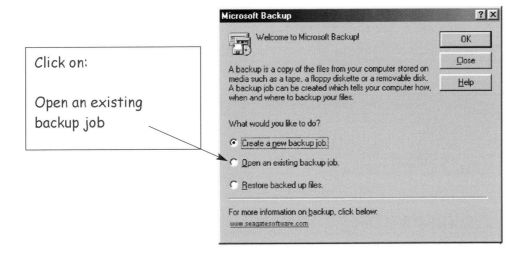

Choose the option for the backup that has been set up and click on Open.

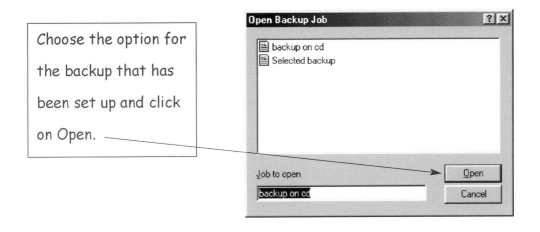

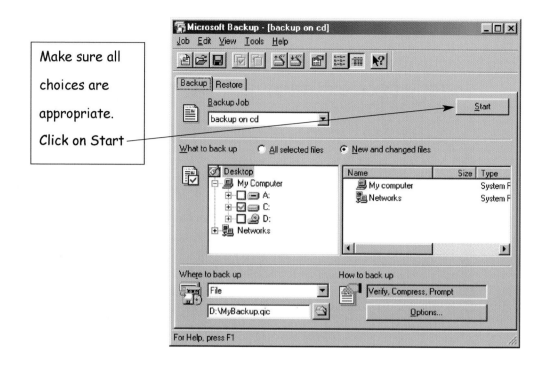

Make sure all choices are appropriate.

Click on Start

The following menus will appear:

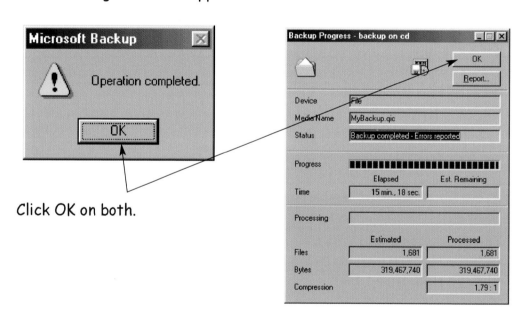

Click OK on both.

# Maintenance: viruses

A virus on a computer can be a nuisance, and destructive, so ensure that there is virus software on the computer. Never use a floppy or CD Rom that has been used in another computer, without first checking that it is virus free. To do this, click on the icon for the virus software and locate the option that allows for this action.

Make sure that the virus software is working all the time so that it is continually looking for viruses on the system. Many Local Education Authorities have their own firewall protection and virus software, so if networked into the LEA this should work for most schools.

Make sure the virus software is updated on a regular basis – usually annually. Regular live updates should be carried out.

Choosing virus software can be a daunting process due to the choice available. For more information check out the following sites:

> www.claws-and-paws.com/virus/
> www.virusbtn.com/resources/links/index.xml
> www.research.ibm.com/antivirus

Or look at specific companies such as:

> www.mcafee.com
> www.symantic.com (makers of Norton Antivirus)
> www.sophos.com

## Deleting unwanted files

Make sure that unwanted files are deleted on a regular basis. This is important to keep the memory free. The more information stored on the computer, the slower it will work.

To do this:

Click on Windows Explorer
The icon is either on the Status bar at the bottom of the screen, or under Start, Programs.

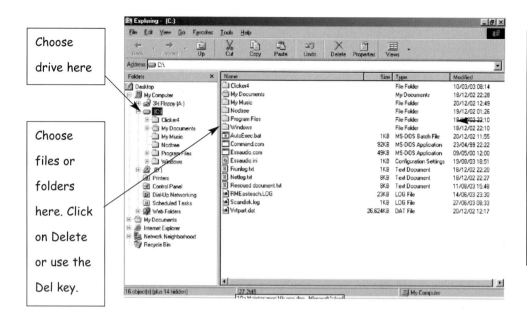

**Choose drive here**

**Choose files or folders here. Click on Delete or use the Del key.**

**Files size and the date/time folders and files were last modified are shown here.**

Look through folders and delete any files no longer needed at least once a term. This saves space on the computer, and time. Large files, or many files, use up memory space and the computer subsequently runs at a slower speed.

This is especially important if the children are saving their work on the hard drive. Ideally each child should have their own disc on which they save all their work. This should be stored in a box by the computer. This is not always possible.

If children's work has to be saved on the hard drive, the procedure for deleting unwanted files will need to be carried out on a weekly basis, depending on the amount the computer is used. Make sure the work is stored where it can easily be located – a folder for each pupil is the ideal, with a shortcut to each folder on the desktop display.

## Optimising the memory space used

When the computer saves a file it does not do this neatly like stacking books on a shelf side by side. Instead it places the file anywhere on the memory where there is sufficient room. This means that there are gaps in the storage space which may not be filled.

Computers have a simple application, called Disk Defragmenter, which can be run to rectify this problem and to free up more space. It works with floppy discs and rewriteable CD ROMs as well.

With a networked system this should only be done by the person maintaining the network e.g. IT co-ordinator, technician etc.

It is important that both the screen saver option and any virus software are disabled while this process is in operation.

Disk Defragmenter:

Click on Start

Programs

Accessories

System Tools

Disk defragmenter

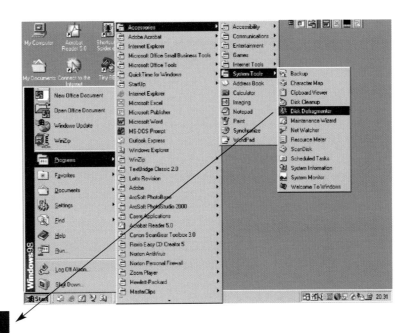

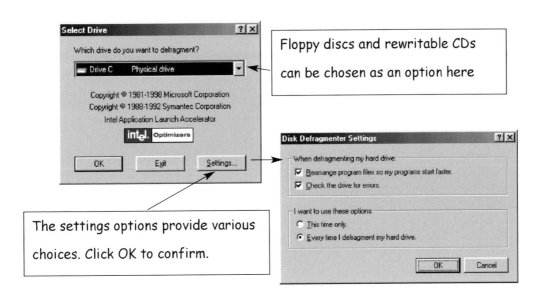

Floppy discs and rewritable CDs can be chosen as an option here

The settings options provide various choices. Click OK to confirm.

Once the process has been started the following display will appear.

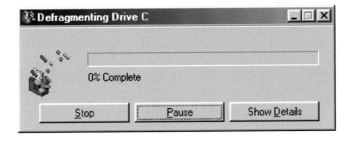

At this point the computer can be left to run through the process. Either turn off the monitor or use the Show Details options in place of the screen saver.

It can take some time – especially the first time this is activated. Done on a regular basis, the computer should be neat and tidy. Again this is a job which could be given to Y5/6 children.

## As a last resort!

Despite all this there will be times when the computer crashes or sticks in a program.

If stuck – don't turn the computer off. First try pressing ctl+alt+del. The following menu should appear:

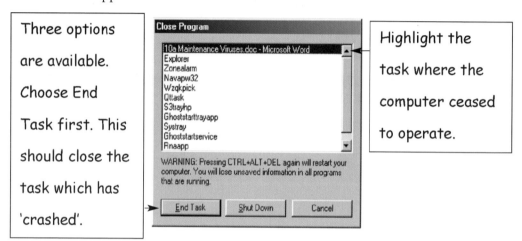

Three options are available. Choose End Task first. This should close the task which has 'crashed'.

Highlight the task where the computer ceased to operate.

Pressing ctl+alt+del again will restart the computer – hopefully work has been saved on a regular basis and little will have been lost!

Only as a VERY last resort should the computer be turned off manually.

## Maintenance checklist:

The following list covers the routine maintenance procedures that should be undertaken on a regular basis in order to prolong the life of the computer.

Daily

● Dusting the screen and keyboard

● Storing CD ROMs and floppy discs correctly

● Keeping the surface area around the computer clean

Weekly

● Running a backup if not on a network

● Running the defragmenter if new files are stored regularly

● Checking for updates on virus software if not on a network

Termly

● Delete any unwanted files

● Run the defragmenter if information is not stored regularly

● Uninstall software that is not used regularly

● Install software for new term